Training Your Horse with Lunge and Long Reins

TRAINING YOUR HORSE *with*
LUNGE & LONG REINS

CHRISTOPHER & VICTORIA COLDREY

The Crowood Press

First published in 1996 by
The Crowood Press Ltd
Ramsbury, Marlborough
Wiltshire SN8 2HR

British Library Cataloguing-in-Publication Data

A catalogue record for this book is available from the British
Library.

ISBN 1 85223 944 1

All photographs by Anthony Reynolds LBIPP, LMPA
Line-drawings by Rhona Knowles

Acknowledgements

Our grateful thanks go to our brilliant staff at Herringswell Bloodstock Centre. The
photographs show clearly why we are so proud of them: not only do they do their job well, they
also really care for the horses and their well-being. It is a lot of extra work to prepare for
photograph sessions, and it was especially hard work for this book because we had to cancel
six times owing to the weather, with everything ready to go on each occasion. This is the third
time that we have teamed up with Anthony Reynolds LBIPP, LMPA whose marvellous
photographs make so much difference to the result. Working with someone so professional,
experienced and imaginative makes it all seem terribly easy.

Typeset by Footnote Graphics, Warminster, Wiltshire
Printed and bound in Great Britain by WBC Book Manufacturers,
Bridgend, Mid Glamorgan

Contents

Foreword

The arts of lungeing and long-reining are fascinating. They give us the unique opportunity to study the horse and observe his gaits, balance and natural flair independent of, and unencumbered by, the rider. With careful discipline, and through displaying understanding of a horse's reactions during training, we can enhance his ability and develop his paces.

This comprehensive book offers a fresh insight into the subject. Christopher and Victoria Coldrey have used their years of experience to put together a very full explanation of how to lunge and long rein effectively, both for the purpose of breaking/starting horses and for improving or correcting more experienced ones. Throughout, they stress the importance of assessing and monitoring the horse's reactions to each set of circumstances, and show that this is a key factor in determining the speed at which the horse can be expected to progress. The horse's physiological make-up, and the ways in which it can be enhanced, are also considered and taken into account

It is very often said, especially within the context of horse training, that 'many roads lead to Rome'; the important thing is to know where Rome is. This book shares with us alternative methods to those laid down in some more formal textbooks, and the reasons for offering these alternatives are clearly explained. If you are totally unfamiliar with lungeing or long reining, you are of course advised to seek experienced, personal guidance before embarking on the task alone, especially if your horse is young or inexperienced. But this well-illustrated book provides excellent guidance, and the equipment and facilities needed are clearly explained. I would recommend it to any keen horse trainer, amateur or professional.

As a trainer of instructors, I often say to my pupils, 'Think of all the knowledge you have as being part of a tool kit, together with your practical expertise. Keep it all together and utilize whichever tool is appropriate in any given situation.' I shall keep Christopher and Victoria's book in my 'tool kit', and I expect it to be very useful.

Jane Houghton-Brown, F.B.H.S.,
1996

Introduction

The motto for this book is 'There is no such thing as a bad horse, only bad trainers'. This is almost, but not absolutely true because you can go on from there and aver that if a horse is not going as well as it should within the limitations of its own potential, in nine cases out of ten there is a physical reason for it. If you, or your vet, or your physiotherapist can find what is wrong, treat it and get it right, the problem will be solved and your horse will be able to realize his lost potential again.

The worst thing that you can do when your horse is going badly, or resisting, or going stiffly, is to increase the work. No, find out what is wrong, fix it, and then start work again slowly and build up gradually to full performance. Later on there is a chapter on the common causes of horses going off their peak performance which will help any trainer when things are less than perfect.

So, before you work your horse you need to make certain of two things: first, that he is right in himself; and second, that you understand what you are doing. You must be a good trainer at whatever level you want to train your horse. That is the purpose of this book: to help you become an expert at lungeing or long reining. To succeed you must understand why you are doing it, know how to do it, be able to see and feel whether your horse is going correctly or not, and

to put things right as soon as, if not before, they have started to go wrong.

In our book *Breaking and Training Young Horses* we wrote, mostly, about breaking in young racehorses, that is yearlings and two-year-olds. In this book, although lungeing and long reining youngsters is touched on, we are more concerned with the non-racehorse, namely the competition and pleasure horse. The idea is to help riders – our readers – to get the best from their horses and to show how lungeing and long reining can help to achieve this.

Everything we have written concerns the pursuit of excellence. If you keep a horse just to get pleasure from riding him – which is, actually, the point of the whole thing – that pleasure will only be enhanced by beautiful training. I learned this forty years ago, when I was in the army in Germany, from our German riding master, von Levetzow; he had been on the staff of the German cavalry school in Hanover. The most important thing I gleaned from him was that your horse is probably only ridden for an hour or so each day and therefore you cannot afford to waste any of that short time: for that hour you must give yourself completely to your horse. Your concentration will be richly rewarded when he returns your work a hundred-fold by giving you a lovely ride. Concentration is the true hallmark of the professional: it is the sure way to achieve a good result.

So if a thing is worth doing at all, it is worth doing well. If your interest in lungeing and long reining is mostly concerned with breaking in young horses, I suggest that *Breaking and Training Young Horses* is more appropriate for you. If, however, you want to use the reins for exercise, schooling or rehabilitation work, then I hope that this will fit the bill. In any case, what you 'read, mark, learn and inwardly digest' from these pages will enable you to do a better job with more confidence and so improve your horse's attitude and performance.

For the purposes of simplicity throughout the text, the word 'man' means mankind or *homo sapiens* and includes both sexes. Similarly when talking about a horse, the word 'he' is used in preference to 'it', which is too impersonal. In this case 'he' refers to either sex, too.

The excellent photographs are taken by Anthony Reynolds and we have deliberately not used any highly trained horses. Most of the pictures are of Herringswell Henry, a seven-year-old who was in training as a racehorse but is now being reschooled to become a competition horse. He is very onward bound, so lungeing and long reining have played an important part in 'switching him off'. However both Henry, and all the others pictured here, are just the sort of animals that readers are likely to encounter.

1 When and Why to Lunge

Lungeing has very many different purposes and uses. It is impossible to keep horses without having to lunge them sometimes, so it is obviously sensible to be able to do it properly and get the maximum benefit for your trouble. There are many occasions when lungeing is useful, desirable or essential.

EXERCISE

There are some days when you either don't want to, or can't ride and when, perhaps, you do not want someone else to ride your horse. On these days, half an hour or so on the lunge makes an excellent substitute: to get your horse

Fig 1   Herringswell Henry stretching and relaxing after working on the lunge.

going in a relaxed manner, soft and flexible, in both directions, to stretch the neck forwards and downwards and so lengthen and relax the muscles of the back and along the topsides of the neck without the hindrance and weight of saddle and rider is really good therapy, especially for a horse in hard work.

VARIETY

It is terribly important to give your horse as much variety in his work as is consistent with training him for whatever is his main job, whether this will be racing, eventing, dressage or showjumping. When I had showjumpers and eventers, I varied their work as much as I possibly could. A typical week's programme might go something like this:

Monday	Flatwork and gymnastic jumping exercises.
Tuesday	Cross-country bravery day – fording streams, ditches, bursting through thickets and so on.
Wednesday	Flatwork and gymnastic jumping exercises.
Thursday	**Lunge**.
Friday	Balance training: walk and trot over uneven terrain on a long rein.
Saturday	Flatwork and jumping.
Sunday	Rest.

Lungeing plays an excellent part in this variety. It helps the fit horse to unwind without losing anything.

Incidentally, it never does a horse that is in hard work any harm to have a day off. In the case of a young horse whose mind is under strain just as much as his body, we have found that a day off does nothing but good, especially if he can be turned out in a pleasant, sheltered grass field for a few hours.

AFTER INJURY

A horse that has been box-rested for a long period following injury will have become very weak, and will have to be brought back quite slowly when he first starts exercising. This is done most effectively on the lunge when his back muscles can be built up until he is ready to take the weight of the rider again.

We think that following a leg injury, the horse walker is even better than lungeing because it is easier to control the pace; it is then less likely that your horse will inflame the injury by going too fast.

A horse with a sore back cannot be ridden and so can be kept fit on the lunge – although there is no excuse for giving him such a sore in the first place.

'JOINING UP'

This is an expression introduced to us by Monty Roberts, the American horseman who made such an impression with his breaking demonstrations and his articulate description of what he was doing. His exposition of 'joining up' – the bonding between a man and his horse – gave everyone a lot to think about, and we learned from that.

To be inside a lunge ring with a horse, especially alone with the horse, is a great opportunity to increase mutual understanding; to get on together through the voice, through hands on the

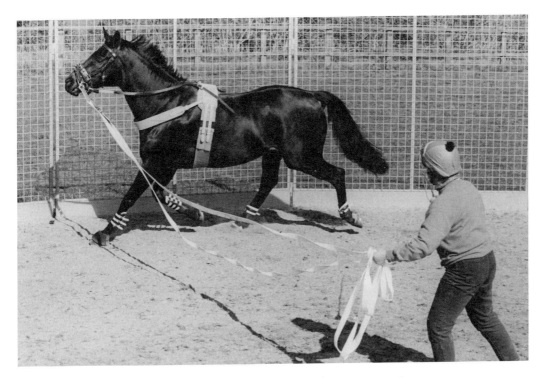

Fig 2   Thinking up some mischief. He is keeping an eye on Victoria and calculating whether he can get away with a quick cut across the lunge ring . . .

Fig 3   . . . and decides it is worth a try. Note that in the first picture Victoria is moving towards her horse to keep him out but he gets in front of her and makes a dash for it.

Figs 4 and 5   The reins have got too long, and before you know what has hit you, he has got a foot over the rein and turned in towards you and is laughing at you.

12

Fig 6   The pleasures of perfect harmony between horse and lunger:
understanding, enjoyment and concentration.

reins and above all through the body language that comes from the posture and placing of the lunger as both of you advance and retreat. The body language of the horse, too, is explicit: he turns away and looks out of the ring, he observes you out of the corner of his eye, he tries it on by coming off the track and dashing with a short cut across the ring; or sometimes the moment you lose concentration or put your body in the wrong position, he has turned round and is going the other way, before you can do anything about it. But it is incredibly rewarding when, after a few days, you are working in perfect harmony, understanding one another, enjoying the team-work and, through concentration, achieving results you wouldn't have dared dream about only a short time before. One of the greatest joys of horsemanship is the development of this partnership so that you only have to *think* something for the horse to do it. Good style on a horse has been defined as 'the maximum effect with the minimum movement from the rider'. It comes only from such a partnership, and the lunge ring is one of the best places to establish it.

13

SUPPLING UP

You will often see competitors lungeing their horses before they get on them to compete. This is to make them supple and relaxed and to put their body and mind in a better state of readiness for the greater demands which are shortly going to be asked of them. It is essential to increase the amount of oxygen getting into the bloodstream and, by quickening the heartbeat, muscles obtain that extra oxygen just when they need it most. Watch athletes preparing themselves for a race: they shake themselves to free up the muscles, they bend and stretch to become supple, they jog on the spot to get the blood flowing and to warm up the muscles that are soon going to be under stress.

This is what lungeing does for a horse in the same circumstances. But note what the athlete does immediately before the start: *concentrates* – everything is focused, and nothing can now disturb his concentration on the only thing that matters, which is to win. The same applies to the rider and, because of the partnership between them, to the horse.

BREAKING IN
(see *Breaking and Training Young Horses*)

Lungeing is an essential part of breaking in, and you cannot progress until your horse is going nicely on the lunge. It is also an essential part of joining up: it is your opportunity to establish that essential rapport which will make the rest of the breaking process infinitely easier and more enjoyable.

TRAINING THE RIDER

Lungeing the rider is a marvellous way of establishing an independent seat; it can be done either with or without a saddle. The sport of vaulting, fairly new to Britain and to the FEI, is a great way for children to start off. They learn to adapt all their movements to those of the horse, and so cultivate a sense of balance and rhythm, two attributes vital to the good horseman. Music, gymnastics and riding have an enormous amount in common because they all demand perfect timing and rhythm; a favourite maxim is: 'Show me someone who can't dance in time with the music, and I will show you someone who will never be a great rider.'

It is absolutely essential that a really steady, reliable horse is used when lungeing a rider, or accidents are inevitable. A novice is bound to bounce about on the horse's back and be pretty unbalanced, and you need a long-suffering animal to put up with this treatment until the rider gets the feel of it. The euphoria when he suddenly finds he can keep his seat glued to the saddle and move easily in harmony with the horse is hugely satisfying. It is a feeling of achievement and understanding, and is a giant stride towards becoming a real horseman.

FINDING OUT ABOUT YOUR HORSE

There is much to be learned from watching your horse on the lunge. You can see how he moves, study his action and watch the development of his muscles, especially of his neck, back and quarters; none of these can be seen from his back.

Fig 7   Vaulting: a wonderful sport, in particular to give children a sense of rhythm, timing and balance; and to teach them to jump on again if they fall off! They are using a Fulmer snaffle with the lunge rein attached directly onto the bit.

Perhaps the best case for lungeing that I have read comes from Col. Waldemar Seunig's book *Horsemanship*:

Lungeing is an excellent way of strengthening the confidence of the young horse in man – even outside the stable – and quieting it down. It also provides the unconstrained movement it requires to keep healthy. Untroubled by the muscular aches that the rider's weight would cause it at first, it will reach forward for the bit more easily under the mild urging of the whip, rediscovering in this suppleness the balanced long strides characteristic of its machinery. In this sense lungeing is also the best corrective method of restoring unconstraint and natural carriage to horses that are psychologically and physically cramped.

(Robert Hale & Company 1958).

SUMMARY

So, there are eight different reasons for

15

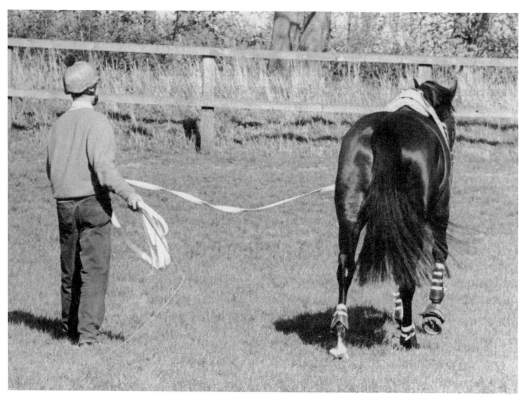

Fig 8   'The best method of restoring unconstraint.' (Seunig)

lungeing, and I have no doubt there are more than that. However, these should certainly be enough to convince you that lungeing is an art that no serious horseman can afford to neglect. But always remember: if you exercise your horse on the lunge and don't concentrate on what you are doing, you are gaining nothing and the horse very little. On the other hand, if you go into the lunge ring with the clear purpose of working on the bonding between you, then both of you will reap the rewards described in this chapter.

2 Preparing your Horse for Lungeing

Before a horse comes in for breaking there are a number of things he should be taught, and the sooner in his life that he learns these things, the easier his life is going to be – not only for him, but also for those who look after him and ride him. This concept was perfectly described by Xenophon, who wrote on this subject twenty-three centuries ago:

See to it that the colt be kind, used to the hand, and fond of men when he is put out to the horse-breaker. He is generally made so at home and by the groom, if the man knows how to manage, so that solitude means to the colt hunger and thirst and teasing horseflies, while food, drink and relief from pain come from man. For if this be done, colts must not only love men, but even long for them. Then, too, the horse should be stroked in the places which he most likes to have handled; that is, where the hair is thickest, and where he is least able to help himself if anything hurts him. The groom should also be directed to lead him through crowds, and to make him familiar with all sorts of sights and all sorts of noises. Whenever the colt is frightened at any of them, he should be taught, not by irritating but by soothing him, that there is nothing to fear. It seems to me that this is enough to tell the amateur to do in the matter of horse-breaking.

Xenophon, *The Art Of Horsemanship* translated by M. H. Morgan PHD (J. A. Allen, 1979).

We believe there are six things that a horse should be taught at as early an age as possible. Horses have a wonderful memory, and this is why all early education is so terribly important: if you get it wrong at the beginning, serious damage can easily be done. So it is very much worthwhile to take the time and trouble to make sure that everything goes well, right from the very start.

17

LEARNING TO LEAD

Every horse must learn to be led from the earliest possible time. It is very easy to teach, especially if the mother is brought in at night and put out again in the morning. The first thing to do is to put on a foalslip (a headcollar for a foal); this has a leather strap about a foot long which dangles under the jaw, making it an easy task to catch the foal without frightening him.

WATCH POINT

You *must* check the fitting of the foalslip every day. Foals' heads grow very quickly and if the foalslip gets too tight it will bite through the skin and cause painful sores.

A foal will always walk with his mother, so it is easy to put on a light lead rein and walk along with him. He very soon gets used to this and the leading becomes a routine. This is a good time to start the bonding process between you and your horse; talk to him and stroke him, and praise him as you go along as well as when you are standing with him in the stable.

Once he has got used to being led, you can gradually start to lead him a little bit away from his mother – but never so much as to alarm him. Increase this distance as the time for weaning comes closer, so that when he has been weaned he is still willing to be led by his handler. You should soon be able to take him for walks which both foal and handler can enjoy.

This work will overcome any shyness on the part of the foal so you will be able to handle him and also to catch him in the paddock very easily. As he becomes increasingly biddable he must also learn to lead up for inspection.

LEARNING TO STAND AND TO TROT IN HAND

Once you have the foal or yearling leading up well, he must be taught to stand still and correctly. Then he must learn to trot in hand.

The correct stance is demonstrated in the photograph on page 23: both legs on the side of the horse farthest from the viewer (in this case the off side) are placed inside the legs closest to the viewer (near side), so that in effect the legs on the side nearest the viewer frame the other pair. The weight must be evenly distributed on all four legs. (Incidentally, you will never get an attractive photograph of a standing horse unless the ears are pricked forward.)

To teach him to halt and stand still, you must make it as easy as possible for him. We shall assume that he is already walking quietly and steadily in hand, since there is no point in teaching him to stand if you have not yet achieved this.

As you are leading him along, stop, wait a moment, and then walk on again. Repeat this exercise until you feel that it has become second nature for him to halt when you do. Then prolong the halt for as long as you can without his becoming restive. When you feel that he is settled, stand in front of him as you would if you were standing him up for inspection. Tell him to 'Stand'. If he stands correctly, praise him; if he does not, repeat the command until he does.

Teaching the young horse to trot in hand is quite easy. The thing to remember is not to get in front so that you are dragging him along: you should run beside him, your body level with his head. To do this, it helps if initially you have an assistant who will (tactfully) urge him into trot from behind (and well out of range of the hind feet!).

When you are ready for him to trot, give the voice aid, 'Come on then, T-r-rot', with 'Trot' spoken as a command, and the preliminary given as encouragement and as a means of getting his attention. When he associates the command with the required action (which will usually take two or three days), you can dispense with assistance.

When leading your horse in trot, allow the lead rein to remain slack so that you do not pull at his head, which should be held naturally and straight.

When the horse is both standing and trotting in hand, you can combine the two and achieve a lovely downward transition, through walk, to halt.

STANDING TIED UP

Just as he learns to lead, a foal should learn to stand tied up in the stable without fuss. The best way to introduce this lesson is by putting him on a light lunge rein which you pass through a tie-ring in the stable and back into your hand. You

Fig 10 A rein through the tie-ring to your hand. Teaching a young horse to be groomed.

Fig 11   Tied to the string. Never tie directly onto the ring.

an older horse who won't tie up. Equally it is no good letting a foal or horse, however old or young, get into the habit of pulling back and breaking the string. *On no account be tempted to tie him directly to the ring.* I know of a horse who was thus tied up and who pulled back, slipped, turned upside-down and broke his neck. So start with the lunge rein.

LIFTING UP HIS FEET

For the farrier to work on the feet of an older horse that will not pick up its feet is a nightmare, and it is the main reason why so many farriers have bad backs. From a very early age, foals should learn that no harm will come to them from having their legs touched. Earlier in this chapter we quoted Xenophon who said that 'the horse should be stroked in the places which he most likes to have handled; that is, where the hair is thickest . . .' The legs, however, are thin-haired and the skin close to the bone so they are very sensitive; by nature, therefore, horses do not much like having them touched. So from an early age they must find out that no harm comes to them from this, and that once they are used to it, it is acceptable.

Once the horse will stand and tolerate your hand on his leg, and not flinch from the contact, it becomes a simple matter to get him to pick up his feet. If this is done regularly it will not be long before he offers you his foot as your hand approaches each leg.

Nevertheless, if a yearling is being shod for the first time and gives any indication that he is going to fight the farrier, we always get the vet to give him a tranquillizing injection. The reason for

can then stand beside him and stop him from running backwards by putting a hand on his quarters. Now you can make a fuss of him so he learns to stand and to enjoy being handled. While you do this the mare can be groomed or attended to in any other way. If the foal backs off, let the lunge line out a bit; it is important not to start a battle. Then using your right hand on or behind his quarters, urge him forwards again whilst taking up the slack with your left hand. Before long he will be used to standing connected to the tie-ring and you can tie him up – **but** *never* to the ring itself, always to a loop of string tied to the ring.

Exactly the same method is used for

this is that horses are creatures of habit, and in this situation if they get into the habit of being shod without any fuss or trauma, it is never a problem. If, on the other hand, they are frightened the first time and give the farrier a hard time, you do have a problem and one that can continue for months before the horse settles down and accepts. Exactly the same applies to clipping. Indeed, throughout your horse's life avoid battles by thinking about what you are doing. In this way obedience will be offered willingly and will become second nature.

GROOMING

The horse must gradually become accustomed to being brushed, and once again, the earlier it is started the more readily it is accepted. First with your hand, then with a cloth, then with a soft brush, accustom him to being stroked and praised and made a fuss of. He will love it, provided he is not hurt and only finds it pleasurable.

If a young horse is taught these basic things at an early age, he should become well mannered and biddable; he will like people, and, as Xenophon said, will realize that . . . 'food, drink and relief from pain come from man'.

GENERAL HANDLING AND MANAGEMENT

Do not be tempted to treat the young horse in a tentative way. When you put your hand on him, do so gently but firmly. Always approach him confidently, so giving *him* confidence. Use the

cadence of your voice so he is quite used to people talking around him, even when they talk loudly and laugh. Next he must get used to groups of people around him, and learn not to become upset should they come close to him, or make a lot of noise or want to touch him. It is good policy to have some bantams in the yard, and a few dogs running around; all this is to prepare him so that when he goes out into the big wide world he is confident and not easily alarmed.

This early training really is terribly important because it makes life so much easier later on. I once bought an unbroken seven-year-old that had run wild in a herd all his life except when he had been caught and gelded. When he arrived he was terrified, and pretty dangerous; it was six weeks before we were able to pick up his feet. He eventually became a marvellous junior show-jumper, but only after a long period of hair-raising experiences for us all.

Basically, there are two important points to bear in mind when training horses, and two characteristics that should be instilled into the horse's mind during training. Firstly, horses are very much creatures of habit and they are by nature gregarious. Secondly, they must learn a healthy respect for people, and this respect must blossom into affection.

The Creature of Habit

Going well, being obedient, enjoying his work and accepting all forms of handling – being shod, clipped and boxed – are all matters of habit and once a horse gets used to doing all those things happily, or having them done to him, then he will continue that way indefinitely. But similarly, if he gets into the habit of resisting, being disobedient, refusing, kicking, biting and not accepting handling, he is just as likely to behave in this way indefinitely. That, coupled with his long memory, is why mistakes and neglect should not happen to a horse, especially early in his life.

Gregariousness

In his natural environment the horse is a herd animal. He feels safe in a herd, and if separated only wants to return to his companions. From an early age, therefore, it is important that he is taught, gently but firmly, that in spite of his natural inclinations he must actually do what his rider or handler wants. Thus the trainer must establish a régime of discipline but in such a way that the horse accepts it happily and without question. He must learn that even if he wants to turn left, if his handler wants him to turn right, then he must turn right. If he wants to go fast but his rider wants him to go slower, then he must slow down. If he wants to mooch along but his handler wants greater activity, then he must step out. If he ducks out to the left against his rider's wish he must learn that he will be turned back to the right. And even if he wants to turn into the stable entrance he must walk past it and only turn back and go home when his rider says he can do so. If he wants to leave the arena at a gallop, he must on the contrary walk, go past the exit, turn a circle and walk out quietly on a long rein if that is what his rider wishes.

In this way he will gradually become a well trained horse whose natural inclination will be to do what his rider or handler asks without demur.

Respect and Affection

Horses that have no respect are a danger both to people and to themselves. For this reason young horses, and colts in particular, must learn to stand off from anyone who comes into their box; they must not be allowed to become pushy and over-familiar or they will become dangerous. In fact the bond established between people and their horses can be very deep and strong, and it was even more so, I think, in the days when people depended on their horses for their livelihood or safety. There have been countless tales told of soldiers in bygone wars establishing a quite amazing rapport with their horses, and once such an affection has been established it is amazing what trust a horse will give you. He will jump off what, to him, looks like the edge of the world, in total trust that if you say it is all right it must be so.

> **WATCH POINT**
> Girls must not wear perfume when with colts as it excites them and they become difficult. Fillies and older geldings can be petted as much as you like, however; they thrive on affection.

Although it may not appear to be the case, everything in this chapter is to do with lungeing. You should not start to train your horse either on the lunge, on the long reins or under saddle until these basic criteria have been achieved; and the longer this pattern of discipline is ignored, the more difficult it becomes to establish until, if left too long, the horse becomes untrainable.

WHEN TO START?

It is a mistake to start lungeing at too early a stage. The joints of foals and of yearlings are very fragile, and lasting damage can all too easily occur. Because lungeing must inevitably take place on a circle, more strain is imposed than if the horse were exercised in straight lines. For this reason it is desirable to leave it as late as possible and not to begin lungeing until the breaking-in process is started.

Racehorses are broken in as yearlings between October and the end of the year or early in their two-year-old year; this is because, if they are going to run as two-year-olds, there isn't time to wait any longer. But this breaking needs to be done with care and concentration because at that age it is only too easy to cause damage.

Having said that, however, we believe that the earlier you start the better. We are often asked by people with competition horses when we think they should be broken. Even if a youngster has been bought with a view to becoming an international dressage horse, it is our view that he should be broken as a two-year-old. It is easier, he is much more biddable at that age, he never forgets what he has been taught, and from then on he is better behaved, better to handle, used to and bonded with people and generally more pleasant to deal with. It does him nothing but good, provided that the person who rides him away is light and sympathetic and, especially, has good hands. Such youngsters need only be lightly broken, just so that they can canter well either on their own or in company. Then you can turn them away and forget about them until they are at least three or four years old; you will find that you can take it up again almost as if there had never been a break.

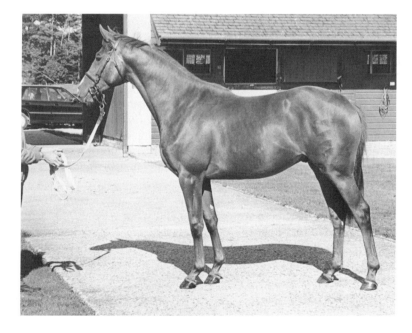

A thoroughbred yearling being taught to stand correctly before being broken in.

3 Some Principles for Lungers

SAFETY

When you have a large yard of valuable horses and even more valuable riders, safety becomes an obsession – and this is no bad thing. We have, as all yards should have, an established safety policy which is given to all members of staff as well as being posted on the tack-room notice-board. For the benefit of stable owners, this safety policy is shown in Appendix 1 at the end of the book; we also think it worth mentioning that a safety policy is in fact a requirement of the Health and Safety Executive.

Many of these safety rules are applicable to someone who is getting a horse ready for lungeing and taking him out to lunge. Obviously if you are lungeing a good old schoolmaster you don't need a body protector, and you are probably right if you think you can lead him about on a headcollar. But nothing infuriates me more than a horse that gets loose unnecessarily. It is surprising how it happens at least once at every show or event you go to, and it is generally because a horse was being led on a headcollar or was left tied up to the side of a horsebox and unattended. In my book this latter practice is unforgivable; even normally calm older horses can readily take fright, especially at a busy, crowded event – as they can in their own stable yard if something untoward happens. So if there is the slightest doubt, lead your horse in a bridle, a cavesson or a Chifney because it could save you from a very nasty accident.

Some other rules that are worth highlighting are:

- Horses should be tied up while being tacked up or skipped out. It is quite a common occurrence to see a horse escape from its stable and get loose in the yard when this is not done.
- We never take a horse on to any road or hard track without knee boots. The boots we use are strapped on below the knee but have an extended front panel so that if a horse should slip or stumble and put his knee on the ground, he kneels on the boot. It has saved many a badly grazed knee, an injury which can be serious and has often kept horses off work for weeks on end.

CONCENTRATION

This is a recurring theme that runs

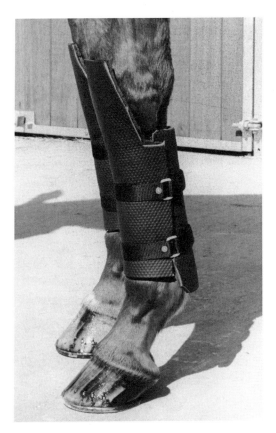

Fig 12 Kneeboots have saved many a grazed knee.

have for lunch. Focus your mind on what you are doing and how to get the very best result.

PLANNING

It follows on that if your lungeing is going to be worth the effort and time it takes to tack up and do the job, you must work out beforehand what you are going to do, for how long and why. I am sure that most people go into the lunge ring with no plan, send the horse round for a few minutes (hopefully in both directions) and then take him in, satisfied that something has been accomplished.

What you should do is this:

• Decide what you want to achieve.
• Plan the stages of work needed to achieve your objective.
• Divide up the time available so that you have a good chance of ending the way you want.

HOW LONG TO WORK?

Working on a circle, especially for an unfit horse, is hard work and the better you, as the lunger, are doing your job the harder it is for him. This is because, by concentrating yourself, you are making the horse concentrate on what he is doing. Also, the slower and more collected his work, more effort he has to make.

When we are starting off young racehorses they only do about ten minutes for the first few days. However, an older horse, even if he is unfit, can probably do twice as long provided that you allow him to walk for about half the total time.

through everything to do with horses. The easiest way to learn it is to work with very young horses: with them, if you take your mind off what you are doing, you are likely to get a sharp and painful reminder. But you must not squander the limited training time you have at your disposal, and every moment must be used for the benefit of your horse.

Thus when lungeing, it is no good just letting the horse go round and round while in spirit you are far away, thinking about how you will spend your lottery winnings or what you are going to

25

Fig 13   Carl Gipson really concentrating on the job!

Fig 14   Getting a tan!

Apart from anything else this is very good training for him and helps to achieve obedience without stress.

You can gradually extend the time and the demands on the horse as he gets fitter. By and large, though, thirty minutes will always be enough.

ONE-SIDEDNESS

Just as people are right- or left-handed, so horses naturally prefer to go in one direction rather than the other – usually to the left. They find it easier because it doesn't strain the muscles. Many people make the serious mistake of obliging the horse to work more on the bad rein than on the good, and in fact this will only make things worse.

The idea is to make the horse ambidextrous; the way to do it is to start with very little work on the difficult rein, and gradually, over a long period, increase it until he is equally at ease in either direction.

If by any chance you find that you cannot get the improvement you want on the difficult rein, you should consult a good equine physiotherapist. Don't forget what we said in the introduction: if the horse is not going as well as it should, there is always a physical reason for it that needs to be put right before you can carry on with your serious work. The reason he doesn't want to go one way is that it hurts.

It is really terribly important to make all horses equally happy on either rein. Take racehorses for example; in this country some racecourses are left-handed and some are right-handed, and it is a dreadful handicap to have a horse that goes much worse on one rein than on the other, a handicap that should have been overcome in the earliest stages of his training. Immortality in a racehorse can be as little as eighteen inches over a mile and a half; therefore one unnecessary change of leg due to discomfort on that rein is all that is needed to make the difference between immortality and oblivion. Or take a horse competing in dressage: in even the simplest novice test, a one-sided horse stands no chance whatsoever.

4 Lunge Rings and Surfaces

Lungeing a green horse without a lunge ring is difficult. The wall of the ring gives the horse something against which to balance himself, as well as helping to keep him on a true circle. Later on it is fine to lunge outside the ring and, of course, essential when jumping on the lunge. But until you have your horse going just as you would like, it is very much easier to use a lunge ring. The other salient advantage of having a ring is that your horse will concentrate a lot better than he will if he is outside with distractions all around him.

The going in a lunge ring is fundamental to its success, and unless you are on very good natural sand, it is really essential to have an all-weather, prepared surface. The trouble with a permanent lunge ring is that even the best of surfaces will deteriorate with too much use and bad weather, and then you are faced with the devil of a job. The ideal is a covered lunge ring.

We use mesh pens, and these are ideal for indoor or outdoor use in winter and in summer. They are easy to move and can be broken down to make two turnout pens. In this respect they are excellent for turning out a horse after injury, their great advantage being that the horse can't get up any sort of speed in the pen and so you avoid that agonising time when your patient gallops around a paddock undoing all the rehabilitation and repair gained during a long period of box rest.

The biggest mistake is to make your lunge ring too small. Ours are always about 15m (50ft) in diameter, and the advantages of a lunge ring of this size are as follows:

• Lungeing on too small a circle puts great strain on a horse's joints, especially the hocks, and is more likely to cause lameness in the form of strain, curbs, thoroughpins and suchlike.
• It is more suitable for backing and riding away than a ring of smaller diameter.
• There is less damage to the ground and so it maintains its surface for longer.
• It is much better to have more room when you start long reining, especially for movements such as changing the rein in an S shape through the centre of the ring.
• Your horse will be more inclined to stay calm because a larger circle is easier for him to perform.

Figs 15 and 16   The covered lunge ring at Tattersalls in Newmarket.

Fig 17 Half the mesh pen used as a turnout pen. Note the 'deliberate mistake' – never turn out a horse without water.

Fig 18 The versatile mesh pens that we use (diameter 15m). A gate which is easy to open from both inside and out is essential.

CHOOSING A SURFACE

Indoors a surface does not, of course, deteriorate anything like as fast as outdoors. The subsurface must be level and free from stones and flint, and rolled tight. A good clay is a fine medium for the indoor subsurface, and a mixture of sand and woodchip makes a good and comparatively inexpensive riding surface, although in time it will break down and become dusty. This can be obviated by using a small quantity of rock salt, raked into the mixture; the effect of the salt is to attract moisture which helps to maintain the texture of the material. Be warned against using rock salt in the winter, however, because too much moisture will cause all sorts of problems.

Choose a surface manufactured by a reputable firm – there are many available. Our outdoor horse-walker track is made of concrete covered by 6in (15cm)

Fig 19 The lunge rings on the Heath at Newmarket; these rings are too small. However, it is a fairly cheap and simple way to set up a lunge ring which can also be moved without too much difficulty.

of surface material; this doesn't sound very deep, but there is no possibility at all of a hoof penetrating anywhere near to the concrete. The same treatment (concrete under surface) would undoubtedly also make a perfect outdoor lunge ring although the edge would have to have a low retaining wall to stop the surface spilling outwards. We have found that there is hardly any depression or track made by the horses, and what there is is only on the very surface

of the material; it takes just a few minutes to rake it level again.

In a yard where lungeing is a daily occurrence it is really hopeless to use natural land, even if it is a very sandy soil. Loam or clay is destroyed in a very short time and involves much time and money to reinstate. It is not only better, but in the long run cheaper to make a really good, well drained arena in the first place.

31

5 Equipment for Lungeing

In this chapter we shall show what equipment you need, some alternatives and how to put it on; in Chapter 6 we will discuss how to use it.

CAVESSON AND REINS

You should lunge off a cavesson and not off either a bridle or a headcollar. The cavessons used throughout this book are

Fig 20   Lungeing and long-reining tack.

Fig 22   *Bridle with lunge rein. This is not recommended.*

Fig 21   *Headcollar with lunge rein. This is not recommended for lungeing. Note the browband (see Watch Point).*

the best, made from leather and steel. They are expensive but they are strong, they fit the horse's head properly, they do not ride up and endanger the eye, and if they are well looked after they will last a lifetime.

We never use nylon for any of our tack. The horse will break before the nylon, and a nylon rein or lead rope can give you a dreadful burn if it is pulled sharply through your hand. The only exception to this rule is that we do use nylon headcollars when swimming horses, because this is one time when the headcollar must not break under any

circumstances. Also, leather becomes slippery when wet which could be dangerous in an emergency.

We use a cavesson with a mouthing bit for a young horse or one with a dry mouth; otherwise in most circumstances we use a Fulmer snaffle so that the bit cannot be pulled through the mouth and pinch. In the photograph (see Fig 20) the mouthing bit is the one on the right with what are called 'keys' attached to the joint of the snaffle; their purpose is that the horse will 'play' with them and so develop a lovely soft, wet mouth. Both the bits in this picture have cheek pieces to stop the bit pulling through the horse's mouth. The ring of the mouthing bit is fixed, and that on the Fulmer is loose.

33

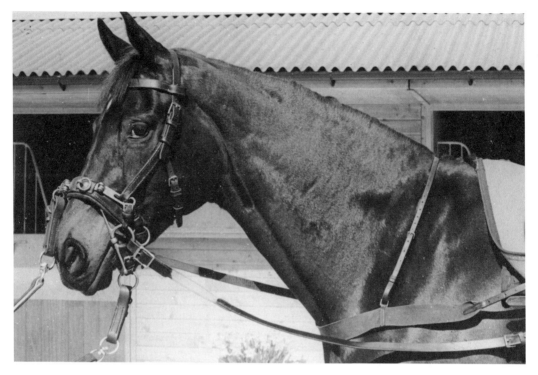

Fig 23   Cavesson without headcollar.

We usually lunge using two reins: the top rein goes on to the ring on the swivel on the top of the noseband, and the bottom rein onto the ring of the connecting leather link that joins the two rings of the snaffle.

With a trained horse the cavesson is put on without the headcollar. But with a horse that you are breaking or one that is wild and frightened it is better to put it on over the headcollar, as is clearly shown in Fig 24. This may seem a lot of trouble but it is very necessary, because if you take the headcollar off and then lose the young or wild horse you could

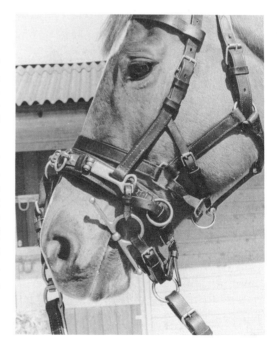

Fig 24   Cavesson with headcollar; notice how the two lunge reins are connected.

34

waste a great deal of time trying to catch him and then put the headcollar on once again.

> **WATCH POINT**
>
> Make sure that if your headcollar has a buckle on the noseband it is above and clear of the the cavesson noseband, otherwise it will pinch (see Fig 24).

You will see that the cavesson has a browband. If your horse is a bit headshy it is probably advisable to leave the browband off for a few days at first; as with shoeing and clipping, it is always better to avoid a battle, so avoid frightening him. In most cases, once he is quite used to having the cavesson put on you will be able to slip the browband on without a problem; with a horse that has had a bad fright, however, this can take several weeks.

So, at this stage we have a horse wearing a cavesson to which we can attach two reins.

> **WATCH POINT**
>
> If he is really difficult, leave a browband on his headcollar. To do this without losing him, put a headcollar with a browband over the one he is wearing already, which you can then slide off. In this way you can keep hold of a difficult customer throughout the change-over.

BOOTS

We have a rule for all horses that if they are shod they must wear brushing boots, behind as well as in front, whenever they are lunged. At this stage your young horse will no doubt be unshod, but a pair of boots should still be put on in front. Now the feet are picked out, the

mane and tail brushed out, and we are ready to go for the first lesson.

> **WATCH POINT**
>
> We make it a rule to pick out the horse's feet both before and after each day's exercise. They will also be done when he is dressed over. So he will be made to pick up his feet for us at least three times a day, and after a few days it will have become second nature.

ROLLER AND BREASTPLATE

Once your horse is lungeing well you will want to use side reins, and to do this you will obviously need either a saddle or a roller and a breastplate. When you lunge with a saddle, always use a breastplate or breastgirth to stop it slipping back. To stop it going forwards, put a chamois leather rinsed in warm water next to the horse's back, to which it will mould itself; then saddle as usual. If you use a roller it need not be expensive; the ones we use are cheap, easy to fit and do the

> **WATCH POINT**
>
> Always avoid any situation in which a girth or surcingle can slip back around the horse's belly. If this happens it becomes a bucking strap or cinch and you have a very dangerous animal on your hands. For this reason the breastplate must be fastened before you attempt to do up the roller. This is also, incidentally, the reason why, when you take a rug off a horse, you always start at the back and work forwards, and when you put a rug on you start at the front and work backwards. I have seen horses run round their box in a frenzy when someone has forgotten to undo the back surcingle.

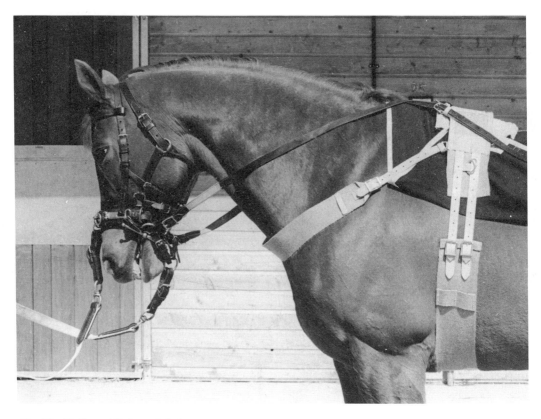

Fig 25   Roller with breastplate.

job perfectly well. We prefer not to use a roller with rings for the reins to run through, and when we come to long reining you will see why.

I do not think it is a part of this book to describe how to put the roller on a young horse you are breaking. However, be warned that if the horse is unbroken, and even more so if he has never been rugged up, *never* just slap a roller on and expect it to be quietly accepted. The process of rollering as a part of breaking is described in detail in Chapter 4 of *Breaking and Training Young Horses*.

EXERCISE SHEET

In cold weather, if your horse is clipped or if you want to hurry the shedding of his coat in the spring, you may decide to lunge with an exercise sheet. This is fitted as shown in Fig 26. Used with a saddle, a sheet will very readily cause a sore back if it is fitted incorrectly: rest it on the horse's bare back with the seams crossing under the saddle and it will eventually rub a hole in his back. We have had several horses sent to us with a sore back and their owners couldn't work out what was causing it.

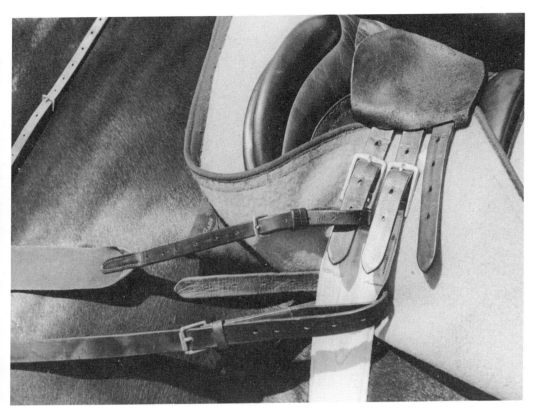

Fig 26   Exercise sheet with saddle, breastplate and side reins attached to the girth.

SIDE REINS

Side reins are of two kinds, with and without elastic. We prefer those with elastic because they are kinder to the horse's mouth if he has not settled. The purpose of side reins is:

• To encourage him to relax his head, neck and jaw.
• To stop him getting his leg over the rein.
• To get him to feel contact on the bars of the mouth from the bit and, as he progresses, to seek that contact.

• To help maintain a constant and correct carriage of the head and neck.

Do not have the side reins at all tight when you start using them; the shorter they are, the more collection you are asking for, and the harder you are asking the horse to work. You can gradually shorten them so as to provide a steady contact, but until you really know what you are doing, err on the side of caution or he will hollow his back and 'break' at the poll.

We attach the side reins to the rings of the bit, pass them across the horse's

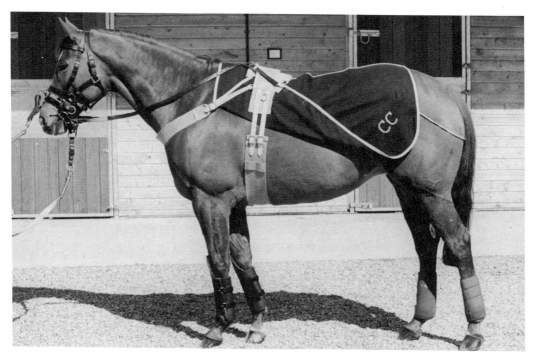

Fig 27   Exercise sheet and roller.

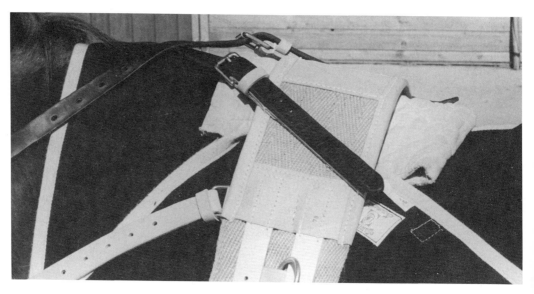

Fig 28   Side reins crossed over the withers and attached to the opposite ring of the roller.

withers and onto the opposite ring of the roller. We do not often use side reins from bit to girth as it tends not to produce a natural head carriage, but rather a forced collection, breaking at the poll. Certainly with a young horse you will get a better and more naturally good head carriage with the side reins crossed over the wither. With an older, more advanced horse you may like to put them directly to the girth (of the saddle or roller) in order to achieve a stronger result and greater collection.

WHIP

Lunge whips need not be expensive; just look after them, and see that there is a lash at the end of the thong. The whole thing, whip, thong and lash, should be long enough to reach the horse when he is moving on the perimeter of your 15m (50ft) circle.

EQUIPMENT FOR THE LUNGER

Headgear

We *always* wear hard hats when lungeing or long reining young horses. Sorry, if you have never done it, but think about it: a kick on the head can kill you or give you terrible brain damage, and it is simply not worth the risk for the sake of the few seconds it takes to put your hat on.

Strong Boots

Footwear with a good grip is essential, especially if conditions are a bit slippery.

Fig 29 Tammy Pick models the gear of the complete lunger.

It makes you look extremely silly (and dirty) if you are pulled over. Also, young horses are very likely to tread on your feet or kick your ankles while leading, and this is not a good idea, especially in cold weather.

Body Protector

This is probably not necessary except when breaking in a youngster or with a particularly difficult horse. When breaking we always make everyone wear body protection. Incidentally, *all* our riders wear body protectors when riding recently broken youngsters or difficult two-year-olds.

Chaps

It is just as well to wear chaps when lungeing a known kicker. They really do offer the lunger a great deal of extra protection.

Gloves

When lungeing youngsters or difficult horses it is always a good idea to wear a pair of string or leather gloves to protect your hands against scalding should your horse take off.

6 First Steps

In this chapter we shall show:

- How to hold the reins
- How to stand in relation to your horse
- How to move in relation to your horse
- How to hold and use your whip
- How to use your voice

HOLDING THE REIN(S)

Having said that we always use two reins, we now say that if you are not used to lungeing you had better start with one. This should be attached to the top ring of the cavesson. However, you

Fig 30 *Lungeing with a single rein onto the ring on the top of the noseband. Side reins crossed over the withers.*

should change to two as soon as you feel able to do so, and there are three main reasons why it is better to use two reins rather than one:

• It is safer. If a rein or buckle breaks or comes undone you still have the other available to you.
• The rein that is attached indirectly to the rings of the bit is a good back-up braking system if and when you need it. You work your horse with the rein on the noseband, with the bit rein kept slack unless you need it.
• The horse becomes used to two reins, and you become used to handling them. It is therefore a much easier transition from lungeing to long reining when the time comes for that.

> **WATCH POINT**
> Don't let the rein get too slack or he will tread on it. If too tight it will stop him or make him tilt his head.

Some people lunge off a snaffle bridle by attaching a single rein to the outside bit-ring, bringing the rein over the head behind the ears, through the inside bit-ring and so to the hand; the result is a mouth which is ruined from the start because if the horse pulls away or runs off, the bit tightens in his mouth and causes pain for all the wrong reasons. No horse should ever be punished by hurting his mouth: it is perfectly easy to discipline him with the top rein of the cavesson without touching his mouth.

It is essential to practise holding the reins before attempting to lunge, and to practise it a great deal. To lead a horse, hold the reins in your right hand below the bit and drop the rest on the ground. Then loop the rein into your right hand.

When all the rein is in your right hand, transfer the looped rein into your left hand and lead the horse with your right hand.

This may sound complicated, but it must become second nature otherwise you can get your hands or fingers badly damaged if they get caught up. The rein must come out of your hand in the right way. Reverse this process to lunge on the right rein.

If you have never done this before, buckle your rein onto a ring on the wall and practise gathering it up as described. Do this first facing one way and then the other so that you become ambidextrous. Once you are happy with one rein, do the same thing with two reins until it has become second nature to pick up both and gather them up exactly as you will when you do it for real.

When you feel you are ready to begin lungeing, start with one rein and an easy-to-lunge older horse and again, make sure you follow the correct technique until it is just an uneventful routine. It is very much easier if you start in a lunge ring. Of course not everyone has this facility and you may have to start in the corner of a paddock. If you find this too difficult you can make yourself a temporary lunge ring out of big straw bales; using a corner made by two hedges is also helpful. Eventually you will want to work the horse out of the lunge ring in straight lines for extended work and over poles and fences; but Rome was not built in a day, and your basic lungeing training should be done in a lunge ring if possible.

The first thing to do once you have sorted out the reins is to lead the horse to the lunge ring holding the reins

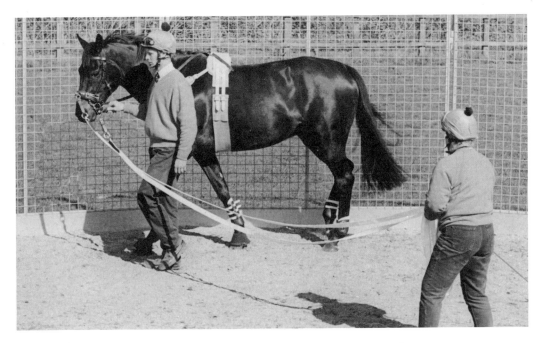

Fig 31   Victoria, with Carl helping by leading the horse until he is used to walking on the circle . . .

Fig 32   Then Carl moves away and . . .

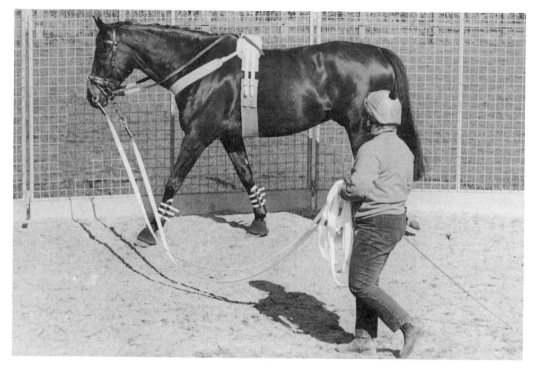

Fig 33 ... disappears, leaving the lunger to carry on.

correctly. Now lead him a couple of times around the ring on a *left*-handed circle: always start to the left because this is the direction he will find easier. If you are nervous or think it is going to be difficult, have a helper to lead the horse while you hold the reins.

HOW TO STAND IN RELATION TO THE HORSE

Once you have led your horse around the ring you can start to lunge him to the left. The rein is coming to the horse from your left hand – or, as we say, you are leading with your left hand. The spare loops of the lunge rein, if any, are in your right hand, as is the whip.

It is absolutely *forbidden* to lead with the wrong hand: you must lead from the left hand on the left rein, and from the right hand on the right rein. If you see someone lungeing using the wrong hand, you know that they are not concentrating and are not bothering to do the job properly; they are being unprofessional! The reason is obvious if you take a good look at Fig 36: if you lead with the wrong hand (the right hand, in this case) your body will be in the wrong position and facing in the wrong direction relative to the horse. In addition, you will not be ready for an emergency should it occur.

Fig 34 Carl standing ready to start lungeing on a left-handed circle. The rein is in his leading (left) hand with the spare loops and whip in his right hand.

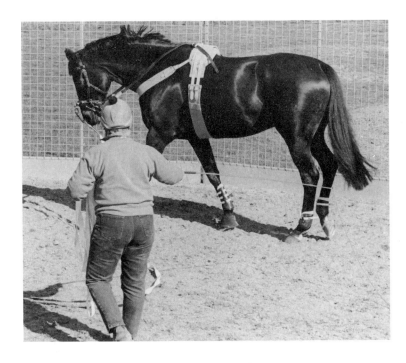

Fig 35 Victoria has the horse between 'hand and leg' (her leading hand and the whip held in the other hand).

When lungeing on two reins, never forget that the tension on the bottom rein must be slacker than that on the top rein to the noseband. The bit rein should only be used to stop or to slow the horse down if he is being silly or inattentive or trying to run away.

The art of lungeing lies *mostly* in the position of your body. When riding we are taught to keep the horse between the leg and the hand. When lungeing, the leading hand corresponds to a rider's hands and the other hand and whip to a rider's legs; your position should be such that the line from your leading hand to the nose of the horse and your whip hand to his tail makes an equal-sided triangle, with your body squarely facing his shoulder.

HOW TO MOVE IN RELATION TO THE HORSE

At first you will probably find it difficult to keep the horse out along the wall of the lunge ring by just standing in the middle, and will have to walk around in a small circle, maintaining your position relative to the horse to keep him moving steadily forwards.

In Fig 37 the lunger's position is shown for three different situations; in each case (as in Fig 36) AC is the left hand and lunge rein, BD is the right hand and whip, and AE is the direction and position of the lunger. In Fig 37, position 1 he is in the same position as in Fig 36; this is the normal position for lungeing when the horse is going steadily along. In position 2 the lunger has moved his body level with the nose of the horse and is facing along the line

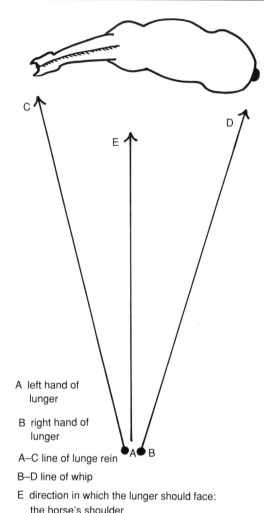

A left hand of lunger

B right hand of lunger

A–C line of lunge rein

B–D line of whip

E direction in which the lunger should face: the horse's shoulder

Fig 36   An equal-sided triangle with the lunger facing the shoulder of the horse. This is position 1 in Fig 37.

of the lunge rein; the distance AC is now greater than BD and the lunger is effectively in front of movement of the horse so he will stop. At the same time point your right hand and whip (BD) at the horse's shoulder so that as he stops he

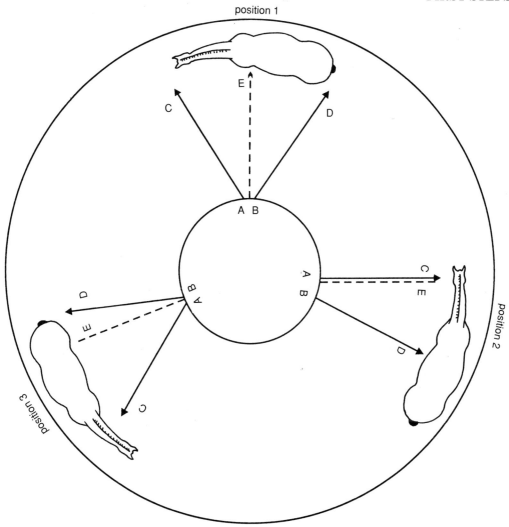

Fig 37 Position 1 *This is the normal position when lungeing.* Position 2 *The lunger is now ahead of the horse. His body language and his voice are saying 'slow down'. The whip BD is will be pointed at the ground and will not be raised up.* Position 3 *Now the lunger is behind the horse, which is being encouraged to go forward more strongly.*

will not turn in and face you, but will stay on the track parallel to the wall of the lunge ring.

In position 3, the lunger has got behind the movement of the horse with the idea of getting him to go forwards more strongly. This requires a lot of practice because in this situation the changes in the positioning of your body will be relative to what you are asking and will indicate different things to the horse. Thus you may want to:

47

- Maintain or increase the tempo and rhythm of the pace
- Extend the stride within the pace

However, you must make sure he doesn't break into a faster pace, and you must be careful to keep him calm and unruffled.

Similarly, if you take a position somewhere between stages 2 and 3 in Fig 37 you can ask for collection. In collection the length of the stride is shortened and the feet are raised higher off the ground. To achieve it you have to increase the impulsion (forward moving power) which comes from behind, whilst at the same time retaining the forward surge that you have created; doing these two things simultaneously should result in a state of collection. However, when you *can* actually do this you are really getting somewhere, and are well on the way to becoming a skilful lunger!

Do not be afraid to move. The idea

Figs 38–40   Herringswell Henry is a young ex-racehorse who is being reschooled to become a competition horse. These pictures perfectly exemplify the body language between lunger and horse: thus Victoria is utterly concentrated on what she is doing, yet she is obviously completely relaxed; there is no tension whatever. In the first picture she is positioning herself behind the horse to keep him moving forwards; as Henry is naturally onward bound, the whip has not been brought into use. In the next picture he is going as she wants, and so she has slowed down her own movement in order to maintain the status quo; if he were not going forwards so freely, she would raise the point of the whip. In the third picture Henry is trotting, Victoria is still and is encouraging him to relax his front end and settle into his rhythm. The side reins ask him to relax into his bit, but are not so tight as to force him into an unnatural posture.

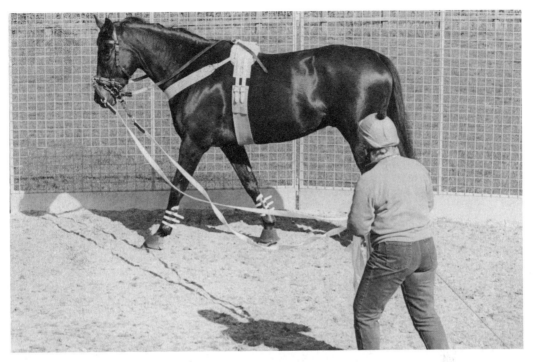

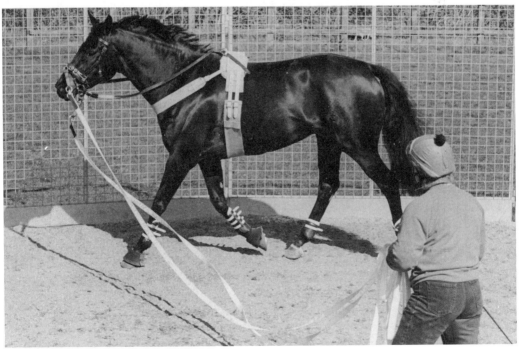

that a good lunger stands in the centre of the circle and pivots on the spot is nonsense, and what really matters is how the horse is going. In order to achieve what has been described you will be constantly on the move, your body and your steps in rhythm with the horse, feeling his state through the reins, concentrating on him and getting him to concentrate on you. These reins are the super-highway along which you send messages to one another.

HOW TO HOLD AND USE YOUR WHIP

The whip is held in the hand other than the leading hand: that is, in the right hand when your horse is going to the left, and vice versa. When the horse is going as you want, the point of the whip should be low – close to the ground – and the thong should be brought up quietly behind the horse in slow half-loops. To make the horse increase his forward movement, raise the point of the whip. To slow him and when you want him to halt, drop the point of the whip (with your body positioned in front of his eye as already described) but as he halts, raise it and point it at his shoulder to keep him standing parallel to the wall and to prevent him turning in to face you.

All this sounds terribly easy, but lungeing is not an exact science and horses are animals, not machines. These suggestions are not rules cast in stone, but are intended to help you use your aids – body, hands, reins, movement, whip and voice – in such a way as to get the best possible result.

> **WATCH POINT**
> Always remember that the purpose of the whip is to guide your horse, and *never* to punish him.

HOW TO USE YOUR VOICE

The commands must be few and simple. It doesn't much matter what you say, but how you say it. We use:

Walk	Canter on
Walk on	Halt
Trot	Good boy/girl
Trot on	

Whatever you say must be clearly communicated and in such a tone as to let the horse know what you want. A brisk 'walk on' will bring him to attention, while 'waaalk' on a lowering and soothing tone will help to steady him. It is good to get an instant response, so when you say 'teeerooo*t*' you want him to trot exactly as you pronounce that final 't'. The same applies when you want him to canter: the command is 'canter – on' and he should strike off as you say 'on'. One of the most important ways to use your voice is to praise the horse. They love applause, and like to know that you really appreciate it when they have done well. So make your voice warm as you say 'good boy' and accompany the praise with a handful of nice fresh grass.

APPLYING THE AIDS

The voice is accompanied with the aids already described. As the horse becomes more attentive and obedient your aids will be less strongly applied until, as with riding, they will be barely perceptible. With a young or a fresh horse, however, you need to have your wits about you all the time. Here are a few tips on applying the aids:

• If the horse is constantly inattentive and disobedient give a hard shake of the lunge rein so that the leather at the end of it slaps him on the nose.
• If he comes off the track and cuts across the true circle do not step away from him, but move towards him pointing the whip at his shoulder to make him go back out. Next time he approaches the place he came off the track, anticipate and think of it before he does so that you prevent it happening again. You do this by getting a little bit ahead of him and by moving out towards the track.
• When asking for extension, raise your leading hand high and forwards, and turn your body so that you are moving almost parallel to him; at the same time raise your whip in the other hand so that you are in effect holding him between the two. Urge him on, keeping your feet in time with his, and send little tremors down the rein to prevent him from breaking. It isn't easy, but it will come to you almost naturally if you have got to the stage when he can be asked for extension.

7 Further Progress

Do not try to progress any further until you have mastered everything described in the previous chapter. That is to say, until you are at ease with handling the reins and whip in all circumstances and until your horse is settled, obedient, going freely forwards and working happily with you. Once you have achieved this you are ready to go on to more interesting and exciting work.

The first thing to do is to identify what we are looking for at walk, trot and canter and to define what the meaning is, at each of those paces, of working, collected and extended strides.

THE HALT

At the halt, the horse should stand attentive, motionless four-square and straight, with the weight evenly distributed over all four legs. The neck should be raised, the poll high and the head slightly in front of the vertical. The horse may quietly champ the bit and should be ready to move off at the slightest indication.

THE WALK

The walk is a marching pace in which the well-defined footfalls follow one another in 'four time'. When the legs on the same side move almost on the same beat the walk tends to become almost a lateral movement. It may become an ambling movement which is a serious fault.

- **Collected Walk** The horse moves resolutely forward with the neck raised and arched. The head is almost vertical and the hind legs are engaged with a good hock action. The pace remains marching and energetic with even, regular footfalls. Each step covers less ground and is higher than at medium (normal) walk because all the joints flex more markedly. The collected walk is shorter than the medium walk, but shows greater activity.

- **Medium Walk** A free, regular and unconstrained walk with a little lengthening. The horse walks energetically but

> **WATCH POINT**
> The extended walk is a very difficult movement. Indeed all extended paces are for advanced horses. Here the word implies only the beginning of such work, and with novice horses you must be satisfied with only as much lengthening of the stride as the horse is ready to produce.

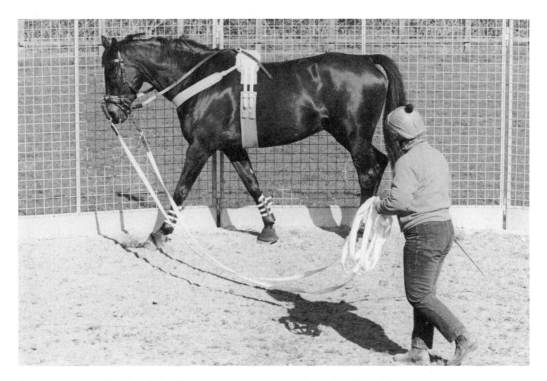

Fig 41   The walk: the off hind is just coming forwards and will be followed by the off fore.

calmly with even and determined steps. The hind feet come to the ground well in front of the footprints of the forefeet.

• **Extended Walk** The horse covers as much ground as possible without haste and without losing the regularity of his steps. The hind feet touch the ground

clearly in front of the footprints of the forefeet. The head and neck are stretched forward, remaining supple at the poll.

• **Free Walk** A relaxed pace in which the horse is allowed complete freedom to lower and stretch out his head and neck.

THE TROT

The trot is a pace of 'two time' on alternate diagonals (near fore/off hind and vice-versa) separated by a moment of suspension. The trot, with free, active

> **WATCH POINT**
> The free walk is a very good exercise, especially for relaxing and developing the long muscles of the neck and back. *But you must keep your wits about you* because, with the head lowered close to the ground, it is *very* easy for the horse to put a leg over the lunge rein.

Fig 42   Henry demonstrates a lengthened stride, with all four feet in the air in that magic moment of suspension. Note how Victoria, having got what she wants, is perfectly relaxed with a lovely soft hand, and uses only the position of her body to maintain the lengthened stride.

and regular steps, should be started off without any hesitation. The quality of the trot depends on the regularity and elasticity of the steps, originating from a supple back and engaged hind quarters, and by the ability to maintain the same rhythm and natural balance, even after a transition from one trot to another.

• **Collected Trot** The horse moves forward with his neck raised and arched. The hocks are well engaged and maintain an energetic impulsion so that the shoulders can move with freedom. The

steps are shorter and the horse is lighter and more mobile.

• **Working Trot** A pace between collected and medium trot. The novice horse, not yet ready for collection, shows himself properly balanced and goes forward with even, elastic steps and a good articulation of the hocks.

• **Medium Trot** This is a pace between the working and the extended trot. It is as much as you will ever want to get on the lunge. The horse goes forward with free and moderately extended steps and an obvious impulsion from the hind quarters. The horse carries his head a little more in front of the vertical than at the working or collected trot, and at the same time lowers his head and neck slightly. The steps should be even and the whole movement balanced and free.

THE CANTER

The canter is a 'three time' pace. At canter to the right the footfalls are as follows: left hind, left diagonal (left fore and right hind simultaneously), right fore, followed by a moment of suspension when all four feet are off the ground before the next stride begins. The canter, with light, cadenced and regular strides should be moved into without hesitation. It should never be allowed to start from a hurried trot. The quality of the canter is judged by the general impression, the regularity and lightness of the pace, the suppleness of the poll and the engagement of the hind quarters with plenty of flexion of the hocks. Rhythm and balance must be maintained.

• **Collected Canter** The horse moves forward with his neck raised and arched. The collected pace is marked by the lightness of the forehand and the engagement of the hind quarters; thus it is characterized by supple, free and mobile shoulders and very active quarters. The horse's strides are shorter than at other canters, but he is lighter and more mobile.

• **Working Canter** This is a pace between the collected and medium canter in which the novice horse, not yet ready for collected work, shows himself properly balanced and goes forward with even, light, cadenced strides and good hock action. This underlines the importance of impulsion originating from the activity of the hind quarters.

• **Medium Canter** The horse goes forward with free, balanced and moderately extended strides with an obvious impulsion from the hind quarters. The head is a little more in front of the vertical than at collected or working canter with a slightly lowered head and neck. The strides should be long and even with the whole movement balanced and unconstrained.

You will never get much extension in the lunge ring and to try to do so will cause excessive strain, especially to the hocks. It is the easiest way to get thoroughpins. Some lengthening of the stride, with no rushing or undue quickening, can be achieved, however. Do not attempt to achieve a medium canter until your working canter is established.

TRANSITIONS

Good transitions from one pace to another are the ultimate test of your success. If they have been developed on the lunge it is a great help when you come to ask for them when you are riding, because on the lunge they are accomplished without pulling at the horse's mouth. Every transition should be as smooth as possible; there should be no shaking of the head; the hocks should be engaged straight away in the new pace; the new pace should be established immediately with no hurrying or panic; and you should be able to feel the rhythm of this new pace straight away.

The easiest transition is from walk to trot, and back again to walk, so establish this first. Once he is doing it as you want, go on to halt and back to walk. This is a bit more difficult, especially making the halt sustained. He must learn to stand still and correctly, although don't expect him to stand for very long before walking on again. When you think you are ready, go from trot to canter transitions; and finally to what I call double transitions, where you leave out an intermediate pace: halt to trot; walk to canter; trot to halt and so on. It is wonderfully exciting when you get a really smooth and steady response.

The question is how to achieve all this, and how to do it well. Doing *more* than just using the ideas explained in the last chapter is very difficult, and the positioning of the body, the use of the reins, whip and voice, indeed all the aids, very much depend on your horse. An onward-bound horse will be different in all those respects from one that is a bit of a slug. Once you have reached this stage as a lunger it is really a matter of your own 'feel' for the horse, and you will know, almost by instinct but backed by knowledge, just what to do and the exact moment to do it.

Anyway, now you know the principles, the aids and how to use them, and exactly what you are seeking to achieve at all paces.

8 Lungeing over Poles and Fences

In all your work over poles and fences use only one rein onto the top of the cavesson. Do not use side reins when jumping.

WALKING OVER POLES

Walking over poles on the ground is the first exercise to ask for, and you can learn a bit about your horse from the way he goes about it. It is *not* good if he rushes impetuously over the poles, knocking them with his feet as he goes; on the other hand if it is obvious that he is trying not to hit them, it is encouraging and a sign that he may have the qualities to make a decent jumper. The most important lesson is for him to look where he is going and to learn to adjust his stride so as to avoid knocking the poles.

Set your poles how you like, and at any odd distances, but not too close to one another. It is as well to put a flower tub or a 'Blok' at the ends of each pole to help keep the horse on the line and reduce the chances of a run-out. (A 'Blok' is a large plastic box on which poles can be balanced; they can be set at three different heights, according to which way

Fig 43   Three Bloks demonstrating the three optional heights.

up the Blok is placed. Bloks are useful for all kinds of schooling over poles, and are used as a safer alternative to cavalletti.)

Start off by lungeing on a circle and, when you are ready, begin to move the horse in straight lines, walking with him and using your body in just the same way as before to keep him going in the direction you want. You can walk a straight line and then circle, then go straight again and so on, each time taking the circle closer to the poles so that, when you are ready, you go straight and walk him as calmly as you can towards

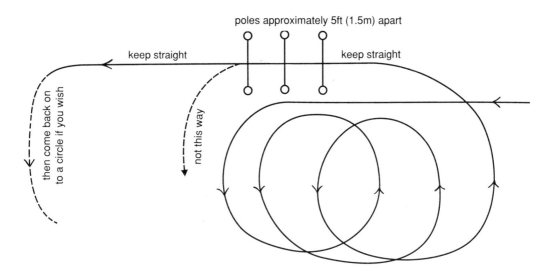

poles approximately 5ft (1.5m) apart

keep straight

keep straight

then come back on
to a circle if you wish

not this way

Fig 44 This line is the one to be taken by the horse over trotting poles on the lunge. It shows a straight approach and finish to the exercise.

the first pole. I suggest you start with just one pole, then two, three or four as you get better at it. Remember that when jumping – and this is really the very first stage of jumping – it is the approach to the fence that matters most. Bring the horse poised, balanced and with sufficient impulsion to the correct point of take-off, and nothing much can go wrong.

So, as you approach the pole on the ground, raise the end of your whip and put yourself in such a position that the horse will not stop but, keeping an easy rhythm, walks calmly over it. In order to keep him going forwards you may have got a bit behind him; now you must quickly, but without upsetting him, get forward again so that he does not swing off the straight line and back on to the circle as soon as he gets to the far side of

the pole. He *must* **keep straight** for a few strides, or he will learn to veer off to the side whenever he lands over a fence. So to prevent him from drifting inwards towards you, it is essential that you step towards him and keep him out on a straight line.

Vary the number of poles and the distances between them. It is fun to have several different sets of poles on the ground around your schooling area; you can then walk around with your horse on the lunge and keep his interest and attention by taking him over the different sets of poles as and when you come to them. It is very good training for both of you, and it helps persuade him that it is easy, and that the best and more enjoyable policy is to do what his handler wants.

Figs 45 and 46 Carl got too far behind and Henry has started to come off the straight line; although Carl has tried to move towards him to keep him out, he has left it too late . . . Henry is obviously not concentrating on the next pole, and the situation is already beyond redemption.

Fig 47   He is still veering towards Carl as he walks over the pole.

TROTTING OVER POLES

When you have mastered the technique of walking over poles you can progress to trotting. The principles are exactly the same, including the way to approach the poles. Again, it is vitally important not to let the horse move in towards you as he comes over the last one.

Start with one, however, and don't let him stop in front of it. That would be really bad training, for it would be *teaching* him that stopping or hesitating in front of a fence was acceptable. Once you have him trotting calmly and rhythmically over one pole you can move on to three. We don't often use two, particularly with an onward-bound horse because he is likely to try and jump

them. When there are three it is more obvious to him that the idea is to trot over them.

You are looking for rhythm. Rhythm is the key to success in most sports, and certainly to all horse sports. Watch a race over fences and see what happens when a horse makes a bad jump: he loses his rhythm completely, and many a race is lost as a result; a tired horse especially takes a long time to regain his rhythm, by which time it is too late. Look at the swimmer who loses the rhythm of his action in the middle of a race: it is quite impossible for him to recover the lost ground.

When trotting over poles the horse will do a classic collected trot, lifting his feet higher, arching his neck and flexing

Fig 48   Now, as he trots over three poles, he has got everything right.

his elbows, knees and hocks to an astonishing degree. This will slow down his tempo slightly, although the forward movement and rhythm of his strides must be retained.

Never do a lengthened trot (medium trot) over poles because it is a contradiction. In lengthened trot the hooves are closer to the ground which, of course, is asking them to hit the poles and is therefore very bad training.

The distance between the poles can vary for any one horse by up to 30cm (1ft). And horses' strides vary considerably, too. On average, however, a distance between trotting poles that the horse will find easy will be about 1.30m (4ft

3in), and you will soon find the setting that your particular horse finds easiest. Once he is doing, say, the standard distance of 1.30m well, you can start to use the 30cm variation; thus you could go as short as 1.15m or as long as 1.45m, always providing he doesn't find it too difficult. The reason for varying the distance is to make him think, and so that he learns to relate the length of his stride to the distance to the pole. This is why working over poles and jumping on the lunge is so beneficial: it teaches the horse to work it all out for himself, and he learns to set himself up for jumping fences. For this reason it is important that riders do not interfere when jump-

Fig 49 Look how Henry uses his elbows, knees and hocks; he doesn't want to touch those poles.

ing small fences, but allow the horse to make his own arrangements. This develops the horse's initiative and his ability to look after himself.

Obviously over trotting poles the smaller the horse or pony the closer the poles must be, but it is surprising, perhaps, that the difference between a horse and a pony is only ever a few inches. It is interesting to find out for yourself what suits your own animal best, and in the process you will learn more about one another.

As in all your work, don't go on for too long. Always finish with a good and suc-

cessful bit of work, and then lavish unstinted praise and affection on the horse so that he knows and is pleased that he has earned your approval. Reward him with a pick of grass, a piece of apple or carrot or a Polo mint.

JUMPING

Before starting to jump it is essential to warm the horse up on the lunge in the normal way, and then over trotting poles to make him concentrate and think about what he is doing.

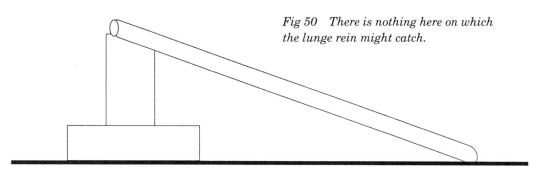

Fig 50   There is nothing here on which the lunge rein might catch.

The first jump will be a little fence of two crossed poles; use the Bloks or similar – not a tall upright – on the side on which you will be standing. Then position a pole so that it slants from the ground to the top of the Blok; this is to make certain that there is nothing on which the lunge rein can catch as the horse jumps the fence. It is also a good idea to have a decent wing on the other side to guide him into the fence. In fact everything must be made as easy and encouraging as possible.

The fence should be jumped from trot. The technique for the approach is exactly the same as for trotting poles (as shown in Fig 44) but with the fence substituted for the poles. It is essential that you keep the horse straight on landing for a couple of strides: *he must not duck in towards you.*

The positioning of your body is vitally important: combined with the other aids it plays an important part in the achieving of your objectives. These are:

• A calm, rhythmical approach with no hesitation at the moment of take-off.
• A straight line into and after the fence.
• Freedom of the head and neck over the fence and on landing.

If you get these right you will give him every opportunity to jump correctly. As regards good technique you are looking for a fluent, rhythmical, flowing jump with a beautiful bascule, that is, a well rounded shape as he arches his head, neck and back over the fence. He should quickly tuck his front legs right up, with pronounced flexion of the knees and fetlock joints; as he goes over the fence the pastern should be at least parallel to the ground. Similarly, the hind legs should fold right up as he clears the fence. One of the great advantages of jumping a horse on the lunge is that it gives you a very good idea as to how good his natural jumping technique is. Without natural jumping ability and a reasonably good natural technique he is unlikely to get to the top as a showjumper. So when you are buying a horse with that purpose in mind it can be a great help to see him jump either on the lunge or loose.

He will soon get the idea, and will be ready to be more adventurous. But never forget that if a horse you are training has a stop at a fence, somewhere along the line you have made a serious mistake. This is true whether the refusal occurs loose, on the lunge or, worse still, when ridden.

Start the next stage with a small vertical fence, then progress to a low parallel, and so on. It is quite impossible to give more specific advice because all horses progress at different rates; also, the experienced trainer can generally ask more, with greater prospect of success, than the novice handler is safe to do. Besides, your horse will tell you when he is ready for a bit more. His jump will be less extravagant and he will become too casual, even bored: this is the time to ask for something new and more demanding. Once he is jumping happily and easily over poles, start to

Fig 51 Henry's first day jumping on the lunge. Carl has given him lovely freedom of the head and neck. He shows a good bascule but his front legs are a bit awry; we shall see what happens when he has had a little bit more experience. The fence is a low parallel which is the best shape for teaching a horse to jump correctly.

Fig 52 Henry has a little buck on landing. This is acceptable as long as it doesn't become a habit. You must avoid pulling his head round in circumstances such as this because the axis joint (where the head joins the neck) can easily become very slightly misaligned, and this can be excruciatingly painful.

introduce new material into the jumps, including fillers such as low walls, pickets, shrubs and others.

Just as you did with the trotting poles, you will have a lot of fun if you can arrange several different fences around your jumping manège and take the horse around them on the lunge, running parallel to him in straight lines between the fences. When you get out of breath you can take a rest by putting him back onto the circle. Make sure that every fence has the sloping pole to guide the lunge rein over the fence without snagging on anything. If you don't have enough Bloks, bales of straw make an adequate substitute.

It is important always to jump a horse on both reins right from the start. He will find it easier on one rein than on the other, but the same rule applies as was described earlier in relation to initial lungeing sessions: lunge more on the good rein than the difficult one. Ask for less when jumping on the rein he finds awkward, and only gradually increase

Figs 53 and 54 Henry over an ascending parallel. In the first picture folding his front legs quite well, and in the next one he is tucking up neatly behind. The problem with an ex-hurdler is to get him to jump more slowly and in a better shape.

Fig 55   Finally he is showing a bit of style. In all these three pictures there is a placing pole on the ground about 2.7m in front of the fence.

the work in that direction until he is equally happy both ways. Moreover lungeing over fences is not something that should be done every day. It is but one part of training on the lunge; it gives the horse extra freedom over a fence, and is a good way of assessing his potential. But use it as a break for the horse, rather than as a regular part of his routine.

When you have him jumping well, it is very good training for him to combine trotting poles with a fence to jump. You must still approach the poles in a straight line, and the art is to continue this right through the exercise and after landing. The last of the trotting poles should be about 2.7m (9ft) in front of the fence; start with just one pole at that distance before you progress to three. It is not advisable to try a grid until you are confident about everything so far; obviously the longer the distance involved of all the obstacles over which you are lungeing, the more difficult it will be to start and finish straight. However, nothing ventured, nothing gained, and it is certainly great fun to do.

So, start with the trotting poles, then a gap of 2.7m (9ft) as before, then a small fence (just a cross-pole to start with), then a gap of 3.6m (12ft) which is

67

Figs 56–61   Henry is doing this grid really well (the distances are described above). He trots extravagantly over the trotting poles, jumps well off his hocks over the first little fence and folds up very well indeed over the second part. Note especially how neat he is with his hind legs throughout. Carl keeps pace well; he and the horse are a real team as they go together through the exercise. Henry starts and finishes straight.

Fig 56.

Fig 57.

Fig 58.

Fig 59.

Fig 60.

Fig 61.

Fig 62   Unwinding when work is over so that Henry returns to his stable calm and relaxed.

a bounce distance to another similar fence. These distances will suit a normal-striding horse, and my suggestion would be to err on the. shorter side if yours is the least bit hesitant; after one or two attempts you will be able to set the test at the best and easiest distances for your own horse and purposes. The exercise described above covers a total distance of 11m (36ft), so it will be quite an effort to maintain a straight approach and finish. It means that the horse will have to go in a straight line for at least 25m (77ft)

and you will have to move quite rapidly to keep up!

Always make sure there is nothing that the lunge rein can get caught on the whole way through the exercise.

Whatever exercise you are doing, always finish with a period of relaxation. If you have not been jumping and the horse is still wearing side reins, either lengthen them considerably or take them off; then take the horse for a walk and get him really soft and loose before you take him back to the stable.

9 Lungeing the Rider

For the rider to derive any value from being lunged, it is imperative to have the right horse for the job. He needs to be mature and sensible, and he must be able to maintain a steady pace at trot and canter for quite long periods. And although it is an excellent way for the beginner to develop a correct seat, to be safe it is essential not only to have the right horse, but also a very competent instructor who can teach at the same time as he is lungeing. He must be in complete control, and nobody should even attempt this form of training without first having practised it under supervision from someone well qualified in this particular exercise.

As well as for beginners, being lunged is a wonderful exercise for even the best riders: a deep, strong seat is developed, a wonderful sense of being in rhythm with the horse and, above all, any faults which may have been picked up will disappear. Everyone, no matter how great a rider he may be, needs help from someone on the ground. It is very noticeable around the world the number of competitors who refuse to move without their trainer; this may be expensive, but I'm sure it pays.

Particular care should be taken when tacking up the horse for this exercise. The horse used for vaulting had the lunge rein fitted directly onto the nearside ring of a snaffle (see page 15); however, although a Fulmer snaffle is used so the cheek piece stops the bit from sliding through the mouth and pinching the lips on the other side, this can obviously never be really comfortable, even with a highly trained lungeing horse. We have already discarded the method of lungeing off the bridle where the rein is attached to the bit on the other side and comes over the head through the nearside ring to the lunger's hand. In short when lungeing the rider a cavesson should be used – although the top ring on the noseband will not give sufficient control to be safe. We think therefore that the best and safest system is to use two reins on the cavesson in the way that we have described throughout this book. The rider's reins are buckled directly onto the snaffle, and knotted to prevent them getting in the way; they are only to be picked up when the instructor says so.

The other tack that you need for this work includes side reins on to the girth of the saddle, a neck-strap and boots all round. The neck-strap must be sufficiently long so that the rider can hold on to it without altering the seat the instructor has helped him establish.

The first thing to accomplish with a

Fig 63   Correct seat: there should always be a straight line from the heels, through the point of the hips, the shoulder and the ears of the rider.

novice is to get him sitting comfortably in the correct position. This is best appreciated by referring to the pictures and their captions (see Figs 63–67). However, riding instructors must always remember that good style is purely a matter of function: we only sit in a cer-tain way so that we are best poised to give our horse the maximum help with the least movement; it is not because it is prettier. We have only come to think it looks better because we have been taught that it is the correct way of sitting.

Fig 64   Round back, body tilted forwards.

Fig 65   Leg forward: the 'Old English' hunting seat.

Fig 66   Deep seat with long stirrups. The straight line is still there ...

Fig 67   ... and it is still there with short stirrups for race riding.

Provided the horse is safe enough and is being lunged off two reins, there is no need for the rider to hold the reins. Whilst he is establishing his seat it is better that he uses the neck-strap or the pommel of the saddle to pull himself into the saddle; in this way he will establish a firm and balanced seat which, as he lets go with his hands, is completely independent.

Once the rider is sitting as he should be, he can be sent off around the lunge ring in walk. He must keep his inside hand on the pommel of his saddle and gently pull his weight down into the saddle. I say the inside hand because when riding on a circle the rider tends to lower the outside shoulder; by pulling down with the inside hand this will be corrected. The body must be straight, but even more important it must be relaxed. Whenever the horse stiffens or is disobedient, the response from the novice rider will be to tense every muscle in his body with the result that the balance of his seat is lost, and the horse, feeling his rider is no longer in harmony with him, will get worse, not better.

The moment the rider feels he is losing the steadiness of his seat, he should lean very slightly back and pull himself down into the saddle again until he is once more in rhythm with the swaying movement of the horse's back. In order to enjoy this sense of oneness with the horse, the rider must learn to feel each footfall through his seat bones. When he can identify which foot is striking the

Fig 68   Carl leans slightly back and pulls himself into the saddle.

ground he can be pleased that he is making sound progress.

The horse is just as important a part of the partnership as the rider, and needs to be soft and supple in his movement so as to give as comfortable a ride as possible. It is very difficult to sit deep into the saddle and to relax every muscle in your body when each footfall of your horse jars you from top to toe.

When the rider lets go of the pommel, his hands should hang loosely against his sides; but he should always be ready to grab a hand-hold in an emergency. The instructor must be careful not to give the novice rider too many things to think about at once; he should try to establish just one thing at a time, otherwise the pupil could get into a terrible muddle.

When the pupil is confident at the walk, the lesson can progress to a few gymnastic exercises: swinging one or both arms in big circles; twisting the body in each direction without moving the seat at all; circling one or both feet; swinging one or both legs from the knee down without altering the seat; and so on. The purpose is to make the seat completely independent of the rest of the body, and whatever it happens to be doing. For some of these exercises the rider must take his feet out of the stirrups; these can either be crossed over the front of the saddle, or – if he feels ready to do so – taken off altogether.

Riding without stirrups is a good exercise, but only when the rider feels absolutely ready for it; it is very bad practice to insist on it if he does not and will only make him stiff and tense, and

Figs 69–70   Exercises for the rider on the lunge. All are designed to strengthen the seat, make it independent of the hands and improve the balance of the rider.

Fig 70.

be more likely to upset the horse. This exacerbates the problem, and will put the rider in the wrong position and destroy the independence of his seat totally: only harm will be done.

As in all the work on the lunge, the pupil must ride on both reins, first to the left and then the other way.

Don't go on for too long; this is another way of making the rider unnaturally stiff. A good time to stop is when both rider and instructor feel that some progress has been made; then they will feel they have achieved something. The lesson should not go on to trot until the instructor is happy with the position of his pupil, and confident that he is happy and secure in walk. With a complete

beginner this can take a few days, although a good instructor can make even work at the walk interesting and fun.

When the time comes to start lungeing at trot, the rider must be sure to have the stirrups; he should hold onto the pommel and pull down as already described, and be sitting straight and relaxed with his shoulders square with the horse's ears – the instructor gives the command to trot, and away he goes! To start with he will be doing sitting trot. He should pull his seat right down into the saddle and feel the horse's back through his seat bones. When it comes right, he will suddenly be moving as if he were part of the horse – and a won-

Fig 71   Cantering on the lunge with stirrups crossed. The picture shows to perfection how work on the lunge develops a strong, independent seat.

derful and satisfying moment that is, too. He should gradually relax his hold on the saddle until he has only the lightest touch, and before long he will find he can let go completely. Lo and behold, he now has an independent seat . . . if only for a few moments.

Before many days have passed our pupil will be able to start doing the gymnastic exercises described earlier at the trot, and to ride for short periods without stirrups. When all this has become just an easy routine, and when he feels that he has really developed an independent seat, he is ready to start cantering on the lunge.

It is essential that the horse is steady and dependable for this work; it should not even be attempted if you haven't the right horse for the job. But having said that, if all the ingredients are there, go for it. The rider should only be expected to canter for very short spells to start with, such as a couple of circles, and he should progress only as fast as he is ready for each stage. There is no hurry, and if there is, there shouldn't be.

When cantering it is even more impor-tant that the rider sits still; the seat must be secure and the legs must be steady on the side of the horse. He should use the inside hand to hold him-self down in the saddle, and the upper part of his body will then be able to move easily in rhythm with the movement of the horse's back.

When all this has been successfully mastered, the rider is ready to adven-ture out into the big wide world.

10 When and Why to Long Rein

There are two reasons for long reining. The first is that it is an integral part of the breaking-in process and one that we believe to be absolutely necessary to achieve a good result. The difference between a horse that has been well broken using the long reins, and one that has not, can be spotted immediately: the outline of the well-broken horse is completely different because the correct muscles have been used and developed, and his back, neck and jaw are relaxed; he has therefore learned to carry himself in a soft, rounded shape instead of with a hollow back and an upside-down neck and a head carriage which is too high. The result is, of course, that the well-broken horse gives a much better ride, with a soft back and a good mouth, happily accepting the bit and the feel of the rider's hands and legs.

The second reason is that it is but a simple step to proceed from this stage to much more advanced work; this might be an end in itself and practised only for the pleasure of doing it, rather as some people find it immensely rewarding just to train their horse to a very advanced level without the slightest desire to compete in dressage competitions. Or it may be that a trainer wants to produce a horse capable of giving exhibitions of High School movements in the long reins. This can be seen in its classical form at, for example, the Spanish Riding School, or for pure entertainment at the circus. Incidentally, I was once talking with a famous trainer of circus horses who told me that he never trained a horse for more than twenty minutes at a time on the grounds that a young horse, in particular, can't concentrate for more than a few minutes. So he would take it out up to four times a day for a maximum of twenty minutes at each session, and concentrate on teaching it just one thing at a time.

THE ADVANTAGES OF LONG REINING

Long reining is very much a British way of breaking and until comparatively recent times was little used elsewhere except in Vienna. However, we have been responsible for starting off many hundreds of horses on their careers, and we are utterly convinced that it is by far the best method. The advantages gained from the period a youngster spends in the long reins are these:

• The feel of the reins against his sides is an introduction to the feel of rider's legs, so he is less likely to mind them when he is first ridden.

• The feel of the reins around his hocks accustoms him to having his hind legs touched, and teaches him not to kick at anything including people and other horses.

• It is the first stage in teaching him to steer. The driver has direct contact through the reins to the horse's mouth and can steer the horse using the reins in exactly the same way as if he were riding. He can also move the driven horse sideways by using the reins against its sides, in just the same way as he would use his legs. And just as the rider creates impulsion and controls the swing of the quarters with his legs, so the driver does the same with the reins.

It is easier for the horse, especially a young one, to learn to steer without the encumbrance of the rider's weight.

• The driver has his horse between hand and leg, as it were; and as he gets behind him, impulsion is created so that almost immediately the horse will start to carry himself. Concomitant with self-carriage is a soft, rounded outline, and it is this which is the hallmark of the well-broken horse. Purists will say that true self-carriage takes a long time to achieve, but I can assure them that we see it in the young horses we are breaking every time. It is not forced in any way, and it is one of the wonderful rewards that long reining invariably brings.

• Perhaps the most important benefit of all, however, is that long reining makes

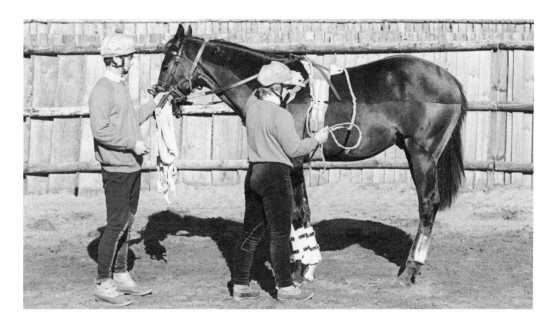

Fig 72   The string is tied to the roller on the far side and gently put over the back of the horse. It is then fed through the ring on the roller on the near side.

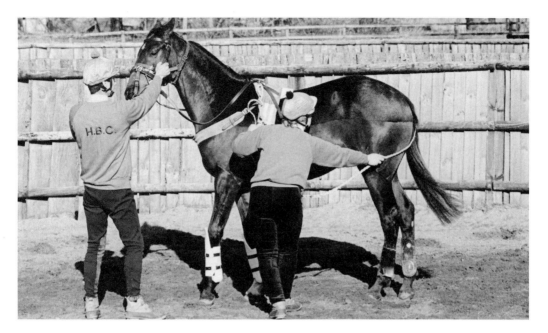

Fig 73   Then it goes around behind the tail, the length is adjusted and a quick release knot is tied at the ring of the roller.

Fig 74   Note the team-work between Victoria and Charles, who now leads on so that the horse gets used to the string before the rein is put round him. If he is going to kick or resist this is when it will happen as he feels the string on his hamstrings as he walks along.

the horse brave. He is facing the world on his own, except that you are there behind, encouraging him and cheering him along, and so he soon gets used to traffic, noises in the hedges, tractors and agricultural machinery of huge proportions, in fact whatever he comes across.

There is one more lesson that should be taught whilst the horse is still on the lunge and before you start driving, and that is to accustom him to the feel of something touching his hocks. We plait a length of rope from old lengths of baling twine and tie this on the girth ring on the roller, then take it around his quarters and back to the girth ring on the other side. When he moves off he will feel the string touch his hocks and will almost certainly kick, so make sure to put boots on him behind to prevent him injuring himself.

When you put the string on for the first time be sure to have someone with you to hold the horse, because he will almost certainly try to run forwards as he will think that something is chasing him. Lead him with the string around his hocks until he is quite accustomed to the feel of it; only when he is absolutely settled should you start lungeing.

Make sure that you tie the string with a quick release knot so you can undo it very quickly in an emergency; as always when training horses, you must be prepared for things to go wrong. If he panics he could get a leg outside the string or, indeed, simply find it all too much and lose his head. As long as you can undo the string with one quick tug no harm will be done and you can quietly start again.

We long rein, therefore, when breaking; we also, of course, put a horse back

> ## WATCH POINT
> - When breaking do not put any shoes on until after rollering. Then only put on front shoes.
> - Do not have hind shoes on when you are long reining, because if you get kicked it will be much more serious.
> - When you are lungeing or long reining make it a rule that a horse that is shod, even if only in front, has boots on. This will reduce the risk of a leg being badly cut if he cavorts about and hits one leg with another.

in the reins and drive him if he comes in for rebreaking. We often recommend that an owner turns his horse away after it has been broken in; when it comes back to us we go through all the stages of breaking again but more quickly, and we invariably find that such horses have forgotten nothing. Also, the work they do on return, apart from reminding them of what they learned before, helps to strengthen them in preparation for the next stage of their training.

The same applies after any lay-off from work, especially if this has been because of injury. In this case it is important to bring the horse back into work gently, and the weight of a rider, especially a big rider, is only an impediment to this. So we would first put such a horse on the horse-walker to get him moving and settled and using all his muscles, and then, depending on the horse and what was planned for him, we might well give him ten days or so in the reins before starting to ride him again.

TEETH AND THEIR INFLUENCE

Whether you are long reining as a stage

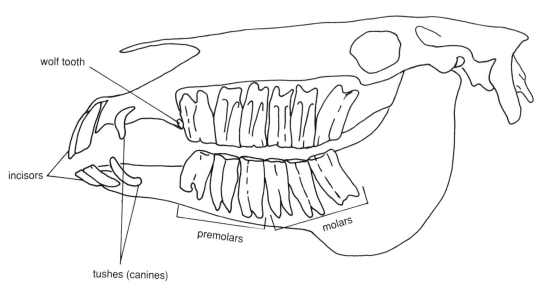

wolf tooth

incisors

tushes (canines)

premolars

molars

Fig 75   The jaw of the horse.

in breaking a horse, or bringing him back into work after a break, it is important to check his teeth before putting a bit in his mouth. If his mouth is uncomfortable or painful, or making the inside of his cheeks sore, he is not going to accept the bit happily. Horses of all ages need their teeth checking regularly, and more often in the years before they have a full mouth, which they have when they are five. If you don't know how to check the mouth yourself, get your vet to do it; it isn't difficult, and it is worth getting him to show you what to look for as it could save him an unnecessary journey in the future.

You are looking for flat, even surfaces on the molars which enable the horse to grind up his food into an easily digestible state; he cannot do this if the sides of the teeth are ridged and sharp. If it actually hurts to eat, he will not eat up and will not be able easily to digest what little he does eat. So you will be wasting your money and he will not be thriving.

Horses lose their milk teeth between three and five years, but sometimes they do not come out easily and are extremely uncomfortable; we have had youngsters whose milk teeth have become painfully embedded in the gum. In such cases you will have a miserable ride on a horse with a very restless head, and one which it is impossible to get going kindly and happily. The milk molars are like caps on top of the permanent teeth, and you can often take them out with your fingers. If they are not easily removable, however, the vet will have them out in a moment with his pincers. An indication that these caps need removing is horribly smelly breath; this is generally a tell-tale sign that you should take action immediately, because it is caused by decaying food lodged between the old

85

milk teeth and the new permanent molars.

If your horse has wolf teeth they should also be taken out. Very many problems with horses stem from the presence of these little teeth which are situated just in front of and touching the front molars. No horse is comfortable with them. They can be quite tricky to get out in one piece, and if they break off the situation is worse than when you started; it is therefore always advisable to call in a vet to do the job, or someone who has had a lot of practice at removing them. So, if you have a problem with your horse's mouth or if he is restless in his head – carrying it tilted to one side, pulling or not accepting the bit – look and see if he has wolf teeth. If he has, get them out before you spoil him. You will be amazed at the result when they have been removed. We have had many difficult horses who have been completely reformed by this simple operation.

I once knew of a dealer who went round looking out for horses that were going badly. The first thing he would do was to look in the mouth, and if the horse had wolf teeth, he would buy him. As soon as he had the teeth out he was able to sell the horse as a reformed character; and what is more, he was absolutely right because the horse *was* reformed.

It always amazes me how often teeth are the root of a problem, and how many good horsemen seem to overlook it as a probable cause of the difficulty. We were recently sent a lovely young horse who had become extremely pushy and difficult; it was also almost impossible to put a bit into his mouth. Our vet took out three caps from his molars, rasped them and removed two wolf teeth, and as soon as he had done so the horse was a new animal and a real joy to have around.

In this chapter we have looked at why we drive our horses in long reins. But I also hope that I have made it quite clear that whatever you do and however well you do it, you will not get a result if the horse is not physically right.

11 Setting Off in the Reins

Starting off a horse in long reins is not a one-man job. It is possible to do it by yourself, but unless your horse is one hundred per cent reliable in every way, it is not a safe thing to do. So always have a helper if you possibly can. If by this time you have done all the lungeing already discussed, you should be perfectly at home with two reins so there should be no need for further practice without a horse. This is how to manage the reins when you first start off:

The left rein: Drop the reins on the ground. Stand on the near side of the horse facing the head, your right shoulder to his shoulder. Hold the left rein in your right hand under the bit and loop the rest of the rein on the ground into your right hand. Transfer all the looped rein into your left hand.

The right rein: Take the right rein under the bit and into your left hand using the first finger of your left hand to keep the two reins separated. Loop the right rein into your left hand until it is looped up tidily. Then separate the two bundles of reins and put them round the horse as shown in the pictures.

Fig 76 shows how to fit the reins and the side reins for driving. For leading, the reins would be fitted to the ring on the noseband and to the ring of the leather bit connector; for long reining, they are buckled onto the rings of the snaffle below the side reins.

Figs 77–80 show how to put the reins around when you are on your own. However, it cannot be overemphasised that you should only ever do this with a trained horse. During the breaking-in process you should start in the lunge ring, though once you have got past that stage you can drive straight out of the stable.

With a young horse, the helper should hold the left rein and the horse's head while the handler negotiates the right rein around the hocks; as he feels it against his legs, watch out in case he lets fly. Fillies are more likely to kick than colts. Then, when you are ready, the helper should lead the horse around the ring (starting to the left, of course) to prevent him running away from the rein. While he walks around it is important to keep the right rein in contact with the hind legs until he is quite settled; then the helper can quietly fade away until you are in sole charge.

To start with, maintain the equal-sided triangle just as you would on the lunge; the only difference is that instead of having a whip in your right hand, you

Fig 76 Fitting the reins and side reins for driving.

now have the outside rein. Both hands are in direct contact with the horse's mouth, and it is vital to bear this in mind all the time. The reins against his sides represent the rider's legs, and the horse must become accustomed to the feel of them there as soon as possible; and instead of resenting them, he must learn to yield to them exactly as he should to pressure from the rider's legs.

You can walk and trot in the lunge ring, and also change the rein: to do this, gradually fall behind the horse, steering him across the ring and then going off the other way as you approach the wall, in a half figure-of-eight. When changing direction use your hands exactly as you would if you were riding: indicate the direction in which you want to go with your inside hand, at the same time

Fig 77 Teresa Ellwood has the left rein looped and ready in her left hand. She shows how the right rein is first looped in the left hand and then transferred to the right hand. In this series of pictures, Teresa is on her own; with a less experienced horse she would have needed someone else to hold the head while she put the reins around.

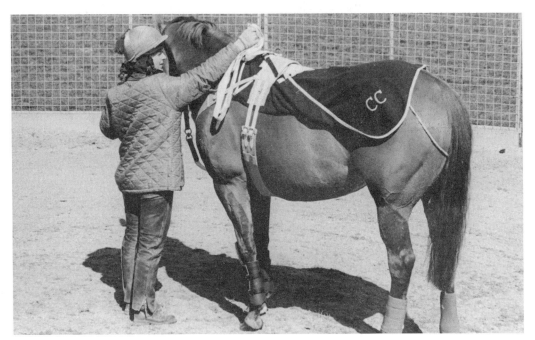

Fig 78 Now, having passed the right rein under the neck (being careful not to pass it through the side rein), she feeds the right rein back . . .

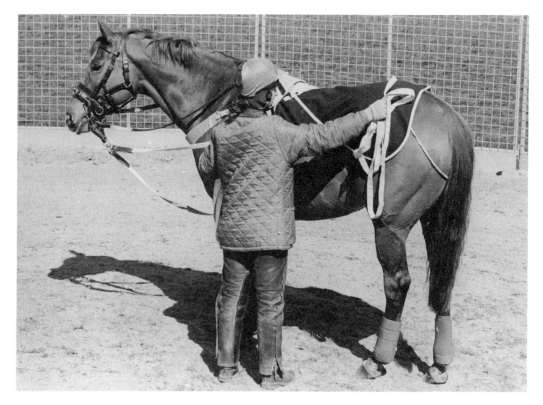

Fig 79 ... and around the quarters. She is holding Persian Measure with the left rein to her left hand.

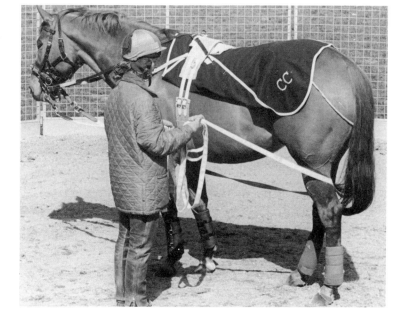

Fig 80 Now she has the mare between her two hands. This picture shows perfectly why it is necessary to prepare for this stage by lungeing with string around the horse's hocks.

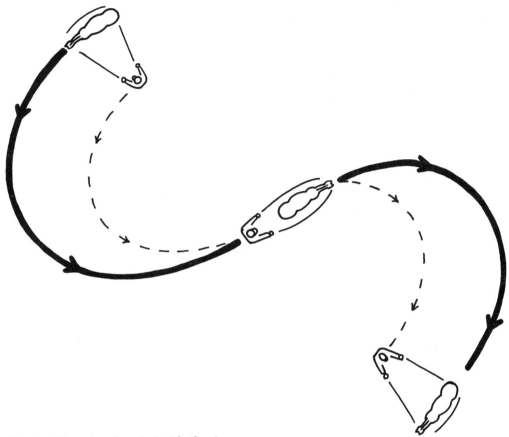

Fig 81 Changing the rein inside the ring.

easing the outside rein to allow the horse to follow his head around the bend. The outside rein will also prevent the quarters from swinging out as he turns. Figs 82–85 show, very nicely, a change of rein in the lunge ring. When you do this while breaking in, always remember that everything that is new to a young horse is also quite stressful. So be content with very little, only do one new thing each day, and as soon as it has been done well, stop. Always be ready to lavish praise and affection upon him, to reward the effort that he has made for you.

When you think he is ready to carry a saddle, put on his tack as shown in Fig 86. When you first put a saddle on any horse, take care! You may get the same reaction as you did when he was first rollered! We start with a light race exercise saddle which does not have a tree and so is hardly felt. The time to beware is when he first moves off; however, if he puts his back up, discipline him with your voice and the top rein on the cavesson. Lead him round the box to let him feel the saddle moving about, until he relaxes again and puts his back down. Then lead him to the lunge ring and

91

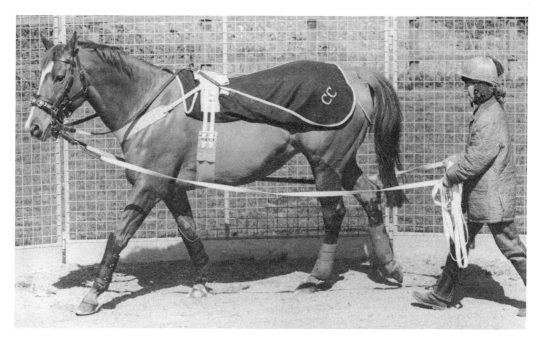

Figs 82 and 83   Starting the change of rein in the lunge ring. Teresa has indicated the new direction with her inside hand and the mare has a lovely bend as she starts her figure-of-eight.

Fig 84 Teresa has crossed to the other side of the mare who is now bending to the right. See how the left rein is eased to allow the bend, but remains in contact to stop the quarters swinging out.

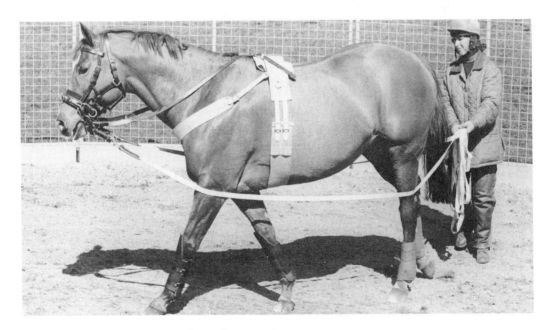

Fig 85 They return to the circle on the new rein.

Fig 86   Now fully tacked up and ready to go for a drive.

change the reins to the driving position, and get him settled down there. Next day you can take him out for a drive.

This is where the most enjoyable part of the whole process begins; you are reaping the rewards for all your hard work. Start where it is quiet and peaceful, and where no untoward and scaring experiences are likely. We have a private track that leads out to a fully railed, secluded field which is a perfect place to start off. Once you feel confident, however, you can be increasingly adventurous until you are happily driving along country lanes and through the village. Even so, it is always advisable to take someone with you in case you get into difficulties or encounter a motorist who comes past too fast.

This is also the important part of training in that it teaches a horse to be brave. When we first took Holly out on

Fig 87 Holly is a very promising three-year-old filly belonging to the successful young event rider from Norfolk, Marie Sleet. Holly is in the reins with Steven Mutton.

Fig 88 Holly comes out of the stables . . .

95

Fig 89   . . . and out on the road through the village of Barrow. As she is still inexperienced she has a 'minder' as well as Steven.

Fig 90   The second time she doesn't in the least worry about the 'SLOW' sign.

Fig 91 A young horse bending down a line of Scotch pines. Not only is he learning to follow the aids – yielding to the leg, following the direction instructed by the inside hand – but also to go bravely through narrow gaps whenever the driver says.

the road, we came on a painted sign across the road saying 'SLOW'. The first time she got to it she arched her neck downwards, almost stopped, blew through her nostrils, studied it with grave suspicion and only then walked across it; coming home she walked straight over it without the slightest hesitation. This says a lot for her courage, *per se*, but also for driving as a way to make a horse brave; Holly's was a classic reaction.

A useful exercise is to bend through a line of trees; this is the outside equivalent of the change of rein in the lunge

Fig 92 The outside rein is against the horse's side to make sure that, as he bends around the trees, his quarters follow in the track of his forehand.

Fig 93   Another narrow gap to negotiate. Excellent bend and lovely expression of concentration from both parties.

Fig 94   He looks down as the surface changes from grass to tarmac at the end of an excellent exercise.

Fig 95   Teresa and Steven drive past Barrow Church. Claire Wright and Joan Melville are on hand in case any help is needed.

ring (see Figs 91–94). It is wonderful training, and points up the idea that the best training for young horses is done without them knowing that they are being schooled. In this case, they have to bend round the trees in order to get to the other side; but the aids that are being given become associated in the horse's subconscious with moving around the inside leg, looking in the direction in which he is going, keeping the hind-quarters following in the track of the forehand.

We like to take young horses out both alone and in a group. It is very necessary that they learn right from the start to do without a lead horse, and long reining is the best way to teach this. It is much

99

Fig 96   *Learning to stand and wait while Victoria opens the gate is all part of the process.*

Fig 97   *There is obviously something interesting going on in the next field, but he walks obediently through the gate and . . .*

100

Fig 98   . . . stands while it is closed.

easier to urge them on from behind than when you are sitting on them. We like to be able to claim that any young horse that we want to send back to the stables will leave the others without any fuss. It is also necessary that they are used to going with other horses in a settled fashion. So, as you can see from the pictures, we send them out in the long reins both on their own and in groups. And all the time we are looking for different things to make them do, so that they become that ideal for their owner, a 'go-anywhere, do-anything horse'. The pictures of the young horse being driven through a gateway are a perfect example of this.

12 Long Reining Systems

Throughout this book we have shown the driving system that we use. Interestingly it is the one used most regularly in Britain, and also in Vienna at the Spanish Riding School, the two places with the longest experience in this art. The overriding advantage of this method, where the reins go directly from the hand of the driver to the bit, is that the unimpeded contact makes for a much more sensitive feel on the reins

and therefore better hands, resulting in a better, softer and kinder mouth.

The other system that is commonly used in Britain is to put the stirrups in such a position as to make – as far as is possible – a straight line from the bit to your hands; the reins are then put through the stirrup on each side. The problem with this is that the driver rarely does have a direct contact with the mouth, and the leverage that occurs

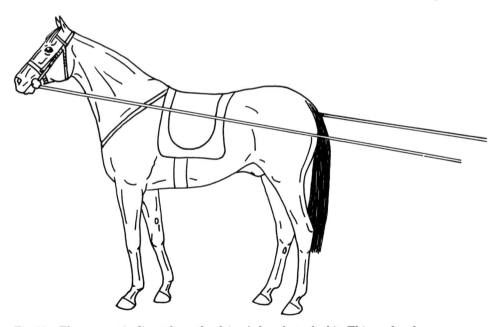

Fig 99   The contact is direct from the driver's hands to the bit. This makes for better hands and a softer, kinder mouth.

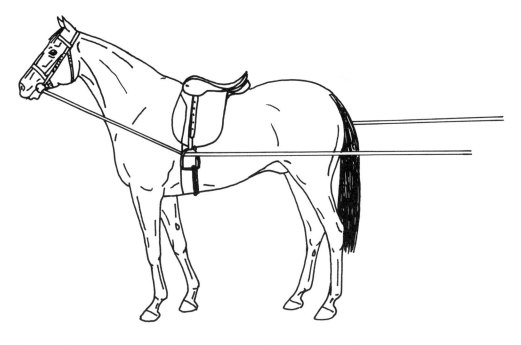

Fig 100   The leverage created by putting the reins through the stirrups bears heavily on the sensitive bars of the mouth.

when he does not, bears heavily on the bars of the mouth; this makes it only too easy to cause the horse to be permanently overbent.

There is a further disadvantage to all the systems that use stirrups or rings to hold the reins in place between the bit and hands: it is that if the horse tries to turn round or runs backwards away from you, the ring or stirrup will act as a lever so that the more you hold on to try and stop the horse, the more you are actually pulling him backwards away from you. The effect is exactly the same as when you take the rein over a horse's head when he is wearing a running martingale: if he is startled or runs back you end up pulling him back even more.

Try it with a long-suffering old pony in the stable; study what happens, and you will see that you have created a pulley.

When long reining through the stirrups a strap passing under the chest stops them from flapping.

All the other systems are based on rollers with rings in different positions. If you decide to use one of these, bear in mind that the more direct the line from the bit to your hands the better. Moreover the Spanish Riding School, which is the one that everyone wants to emulate, uses the method that we recommend, even for the High School work in the reins which is so wonderful.

There is, I must admit, one big advantage in driving from reins coming

Fig 101   In this situation the leverage is intensified. The more you hold on, the more you pull the horse backwards away from you.

through two rings high on the withers: it is that you can do everything standing close to and to one side of the horse. I have seen it used to good effect on very highly advanced horses, although I cannot recommend it for the sort of work about which we have been talking because anything that breaks the straight line between hands and bit increases the leverage on the horse's mouth. This artificially pulls the head down and causes the bit to be more

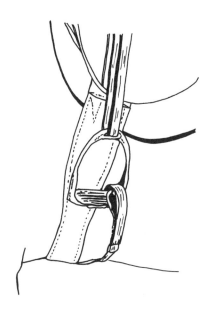

Fig 102   A strap under the chest keeps the stirrups in place and still.

104

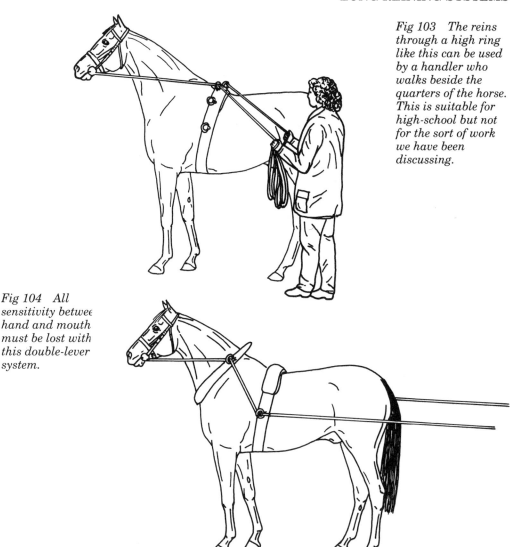

Fig 103 The reins through a high ring like this can be used by a handler who walks beside the quarters of the horse. This is suitable for high-school but not for the sort of work we have been discussing.

Fig 104 All sensitivity betweε hand and mouth must be lost with this double-lever system.

severe, thus leading to a reduction in the mouth's sensitivity. It is like riding with a very short martingale: it may work with certain horses with a particular problem, but is not at all a good idea in normal circumstances.

There is also a system that uses two rollers with rings, one around the neck as well as one in the usual place. The leverage exerted on the horse's mouth here is excessive, and although it might give plenty of control, I should say that it would do more harm than good to the horse. It might, I suppose, be all right for a horse that works in agriculture.

The more natural, and the less forced that your training is, the better the end result is inevitably going to be.

105

13 Getting the Best from your Horse

Getting the best from your horse is really a matter of giving the best to your horse! Be professional in your approach; it really is important to get the very best result from everything you do. It is this pursuit of excellence which will achieve wonderful results for you and your horse. However, you cannot expect success if he is not feeling his best, and there are several reasons that might cause a horse to go less well than you expect.

TEETH

The subject of teeth has already been covered in Chapter 10 in some detail.

WORMS

Most horses carry some sort of worm burden, but if worms are getting more value from the feed you give your horse than he is himself, you are wasting your money. If he is turned out, especially on pasture that has been grazed regularly by horses, he is bound to pick up a lot of worms. Pastures are kept reasonably clean if horses, sheep or cattle are rotated on the grazing, but if the land is 'horse-sick' you need to take professional advice about restoring it.

Horses on grass or coming in from a rest at grass need worming more regularly than those kept in. We worm every six weeks in any case and we use three different wormers in rotation to try to make sure that the whole spectrum is covered.

A bad worm infestation can cause serious colic, so you could even lose your horse if you fail to look after this problem.

FEET

'No foot, no horse' is a truism. Puffy, hot joints, sore shins, loss of action, unwillingness to move forwards freely, as well as actual lameness are all symptoms of foot trouble. If you are not happy that your horse's feet are right you should consult your farrier and/or your vet. Many horses break down and are useless for further serious work because they have been hard ridden when their feet were not properly balanced.

BOREDOM

Boredom can be a problem, especially in small yards where there is little or no company. If the horse can be turned out for a large part of the day he will probably be quite contented on his own; and if you can arrange some company for him it will be a great help: a sheep or a goat or even some bantams and cats will help him retain his interest.

In a larger yard it is not such a problem. We have had many horses restricted to long periods of box rest following injury, but as long as they have plenty to look at and plenty of human as well as equine company they remain amazingly contented. We have made rather a speciality of keeping such horses looking really good even though they are doing nothing. One of the most important factors is for them to have as big a box as you can possibly manage so that they can walk around a bit and not feel too hemmed in.

NOISE

Horses, especially fit, highly strung ones, can become very distressed by loud incessant noise. I once knew a trainer who had a spectacular season; the next year he called the builders in to rebuild his yard and there was no peace whatsoever all day long, with pneumatic drills, concrete lorries and a constant traffic of vehicles and people. The result was that his horses ran really badly – as he remarked disconsolately to me, 'I can walk faster than they can gallop!'

We sincerely believe that peace and quiet in the yard is essential; when we leave the horses after they have had their midday feed, we like them to have complete peace until evening stables begin at four o'clock. The constant noise of engines is very unsettling for them.

PAIN

Many horses which are performing under par would be put right with the attention of a physiotherapist. Unfortunately there are still some vets who are against this sort of treatment, but this really does go against all logic. None of the top human athletes today are without the immediate availability of their chosen physio – and they don't have to perform with someone sitting on the weakest part of their back!

And so it is with horses: a slip getting up in the stable or on the road, too sudden a jump off into canter, a fall over a fence – for a hundred and one reasons a horse may be injured with a strain, a muscle spasm, a joint misaligned, a rib angle and so on. There are several signs which indicate that therapy is needed:

Your horse cringes when you get on: Why? Because it hurts. If he doesn't like a saddle being put on or being mounted, something needs to be done to help him.
It is difficult to rise on one diagonal: Why? Again, because it is more painful on that one. Unfortunately the majority of riders accept this without asking themselves *why* this should be, and just always remain on the same diagonal for the rest of the time they have that horse. But if they had the services of a good equitherapist they would have had a much better ride for all that time.
It is difficult to turn one way: All horses find it easier to go one way than

the other; generally this is to the left as we have already explained. If you cannot overcome this in the way we have described in the lungeing chapters, then there must be a physical reason for it, and this can be located and cured.

Shoes wearing unevenly: This is a symptom that the horse is not 'square'; he is saving some muscle somewhere to avoid pain with the result that he is going crooked. With therapy the pain will go and his action will straighten out.

Flinching: If the horse is over-sensitive anywhere along the length of his spine and flinches from pressure, he needs help. This may have been caused by an ill-fitting saddle, too heavy or clumsy a rider, rolling, almost anything; but fortunately it is easy to remedy.

Bucking: Bucking is likely (but not necessarily) to be caused by pain. The same applies to rearing.

The legal position of equitherapists is tricky. It helps if they have first qualified as human physiotherapists, and the situation is made much easier if your vet agrees to call one in to help. It is perfectly ridiculous that it is not universally accepted as a vital part of equine therapy, as it undoubtedly will be in the course of time.

FEED AND EXERCISE

The important thing to understand is that it is work that makes a horse look good rather than food. Obviously the feeding régime must be excellent, and your horse must have everything that is needed to maintain ideal health and fitness; but you can feed masses of the very best feed and still have a horse that looks like nothing on earth. In my view, many trainers of competition horses of all kinds seem to think that cramming in more protein when their horse is a bit over the top will solve their problem.

If you are sure there is nothing physically wrong with him, then what will build him up is the sort of work that this book has been about. It is so easy to keep your horses looking and feeling wonderful if you are prepared to take the trouble. What is more, it can be done without feeding them to the eyeballs and making them unrideable in the process.

14 Conclusion

We hope that this is not a complicated book. We have tried to express everything in simple, clear terms that are easy to follow and to put into practice. Many so-called experts like to wrap their subject in mystery so that other people think it is too difficult for them. Most things, though, are nothing like as complex as they are made to seem. Common sense and practice are all that is needed to succeed in becoming an expert, and that is what we hope this book will help you to become.

We have not targeted those who already have great knowledge of the subject, but rather ordinary horsemen and women who want to get the very best out of their horses. The main lessons that we have tried to put across are these:

• The importance of concentration on the job in hand.
• If it is worth doing at all it is worth doing well.
• If your horse is not doing his best, look hard for a physical explanation and don't try to force him to do what he is finding difficult.
• Be observant. Spot what is wrong as soon as you see your horse or go into his stable.
• Be unstinting with praise and affection when he has done well.

So, be a good trainer, become an expert and, above all, enjoy the time that you spend in the company of man's first servant, the horse.

Appendix

HERRINGSWELL BLOODSTOCK CENTRE
SAFETY POLICY

1. LOOSE HORSES

1.1   Bottom bolts shut whenever a horse is left in a box.

1.2   No horse to be tied up except to a string loop attached to the tie ring. Under no circumstances is any horse to be tied to a hayrack or anything else except string on a tie ring.

1.3   Horses must be tied up when being saddled and unsaddled and when being mucked out or skipped out.

1.4   No horse to be led out of a box without a bridle or cavesson with reins on and knee boots for road work.

1.5   Paddock and entrance: all gates to be kept closed, and yard gates locked when yard is unattended.

1.6   Sliding partition doors in stallion barn must be properly closed and checked.

2. SAFETY IN BOXES AND YARD

2.1   Visitors are not permitted to approach close to stables or horses. A warning notice to be displayed to this effect at the main entrance.

2.2   No horse to be left tied up unless someone is with it, or special instructions have been given.

2.3   No headcollars to be left tied to the tie ring in the box with a loose horse. No other tack to be left in the box.

2.4   If in doubt no member of staff should enter a box without authority of a senior member of staff. Senior staff must ensure that when necessary one person holds the horse while another does whatever job has to be done.

2.5   All tools must be put away at all times when not in use.

2.6   No string is to be left lying around at any time.

3. TACK

3.1   Tack must be correctly fitted, complete and secure before mounting.

3.2   *All* horses must have knee boots whenever they are ridden or when they are led on the road.

3.3   All staff are responsible for seeing that their tack is clean and in good repair **EVERY DAY**.

3.4   All broken or damaged tack to be handed in for repair or replacement by the rider responsible for it.

4. MOUNTING

4.1   All horses for each lot must come out at the same time.

4.2   Senior staff must ensure that leggers-up are ready to leg up quickly.

4.3   Horses must walk around the gravel yard in a circle until all are ready to go out.

5. CLOTHING

5.1   Correctly fitted hard hats with chin straps secured must be worn by riders at all times and by anyone handling a horse in any stage of breaking.

5.2   Every member of staff is responsible for ensuring that their crash hat is sound and undamaged.

5.3   Body protectors are to be worn by all those riding yearlings and two-year-olds as well as any other horses that are in the process of being broken in.

5.4   Soft shoes (such as trainers) may not be worn in stables with horses. Metal reinforced toe-caps are recommended.

5.5   To minimise the risk of injury in the event of a fall, sleeveless T-shirts may not be worn when riding out.

5.6   Baseball caps with peaks may not be worn on the yard. They impede vision and are often the cause of accidents.

5.7   Long hair must be tied back or plaited or a soft hair band worn to keep hair away from the face. This avoids impaired vision.

6. GENERAL SAFETY

6.1   String must be removed from all bales, tied in a knot, hung on a hook and removed and thrown away straight after each box is finished. Plastic from bales must not be left to blow round the yard.

6.2   When horses leave the stables, doors must be closed or hooked back and lights turned out. Rugs must be folded up and left on the manger or behind the top doors, or undercover if wet.

6.3   No scent/perfume, nail varnish or jewellery, except wedding rings, may be worn at any time when at work.

7. FIRE PRECAUTIONS

7.1   No smoking is allowed at any time.

7.2   All staff must read and understand the Fire Precaution Instruction. The head lad must ensure that this is prominently displayed in the tack room.

8. THE MASTER SAFETY RULE

8.1   Finally *never* take risks or short cuts with these valuable horses. If you are in difficulty, have a problem or don't know what to do, **always** get help or ask senior staff what to do. Be proud of your horse and the yard.

9. ACCIDENTS

9.1   All accidents must be reported to the secretary by the senior member of staff present.

9.2   The secretary is responsible for logging all accidents in the Accident Book and reporting such accidents to the Health and Safety Department when required.

Index